MW00904819

ALPHABET

This section will teach your child to recognize the letters of the alphabet, which is an essential first step in learning to read. Here are some tips to help your child get the most from this section:

- To help your child learn the letters in alphabetical order, encourage your child to work from the beginning to the end of this section.

- Explain to your child that there is an uppercase and lowercase version of each letter.

- Have your child say each letter out loud.

- Encourage your child to pronounce each word that represents each letter. This will help reinforce beginning sounds, another important reading readiness skill.

- The manuscript writing component will give your child an opportunity to practice tracing and writing the letters of the alphabet. The pages include the proper starting points for each letter stroke. Encourage your child to follow the arrows, which will help your child develop legible handwriting.

- Writing lowercase letters is a difficult skill for many children. If tracing the letters with a pencil or crayon is too challenging, encourage your child to trace the letters with his or her finger.

BUZZING AROUND

Connect the dots from **A** to **Z**.
Color the picture.

A B C D E F G H I J K L M N O P Q R S T U V W X Y Z

THE WRITE STUFF!

 Trace the lines from **left** to **right**.

A is for **a**irplane.

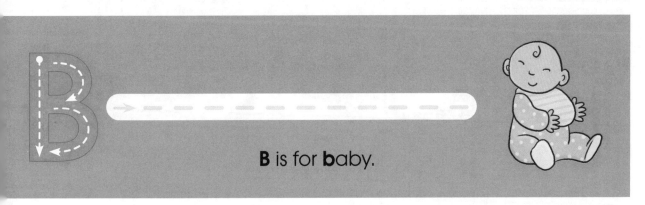

B is for **b**aby.

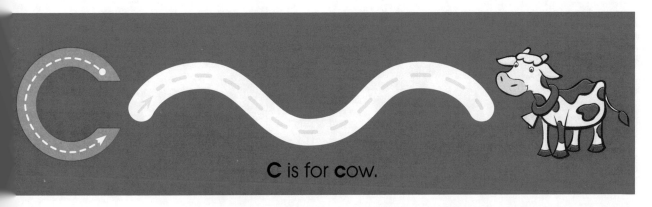

C is for **c**ow.

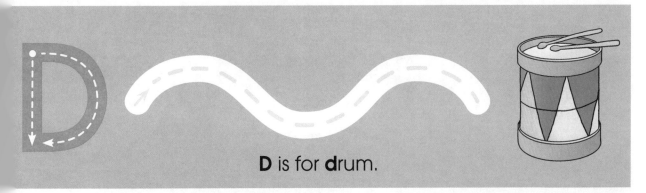

D is for **d**rum.

Trace the lines from **left** to **right**.

E is for **e**nvelope.

F is for **f**lag.

G is for **g**rapes.

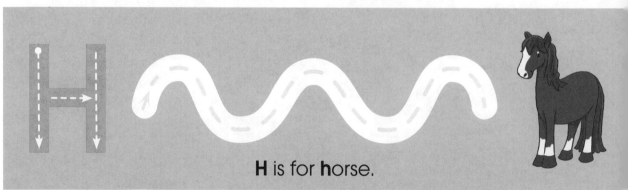

H is for **h**orse.

Trace the lines from **left** to **right**.

I is for **i**gloo.

J is for **j**eep.

K is for **k**itten.

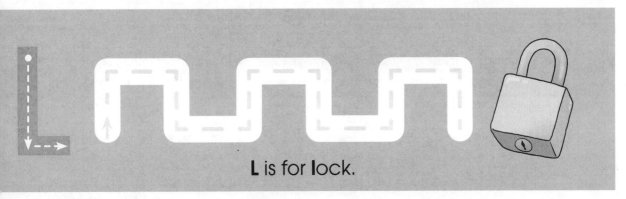

L is for **l**ock.

Trace the lines from **left** to **right**.

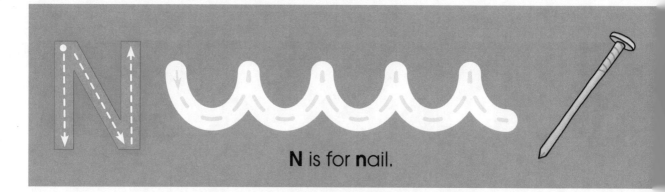

M is for **m**oon.

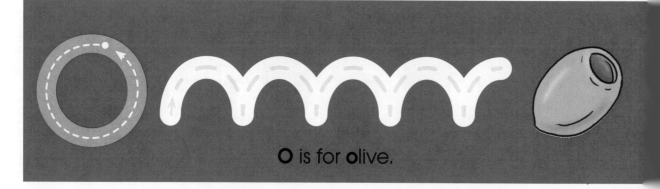

N is for **n**ail.

O is for **o**live.

P is for **p**ear.

Trace the lines from **left** to **right**.

Q is for **q**ueen.

R is for **r**abbit.

S is for **s**pider.

T is for **t**rain.

Trace the lines from **left** to **right**.

U is for **u**nderwear.

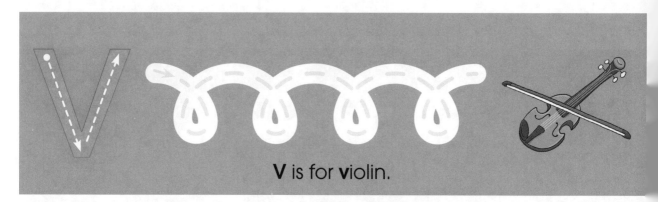

V is for **v**iolin.

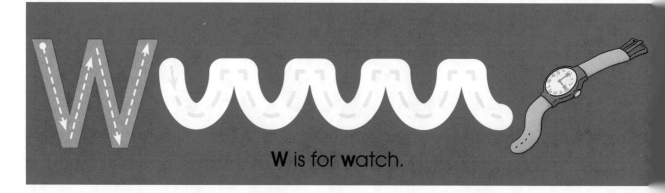

W is for **w**atch.

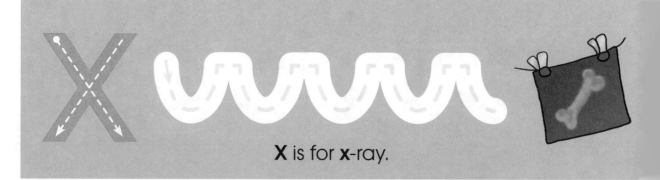

X is for **x**-ray.

Trace the lines from **left** to **right**.

Y is for **y**arn.

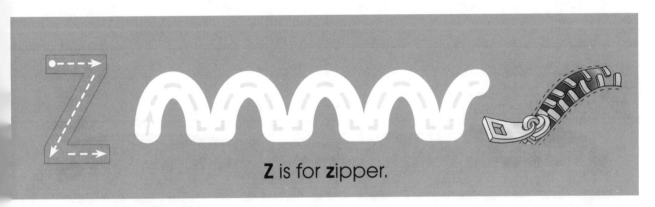

Z is for **z**ipper.

Help **Y** and **Z** find their lunch.
Trace their path.

Trace and write **A**.

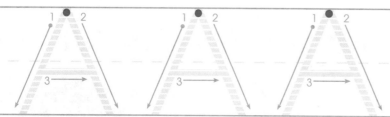

 Trace and write **a**.

 Color the picture.

 Trace the letters to complete the sentence.

A is for airplane.

the pictures that begin with **a**.

 Trace the missing **a** to finish each word.

ant   arrow

apple   ape

Trace and write **B**.

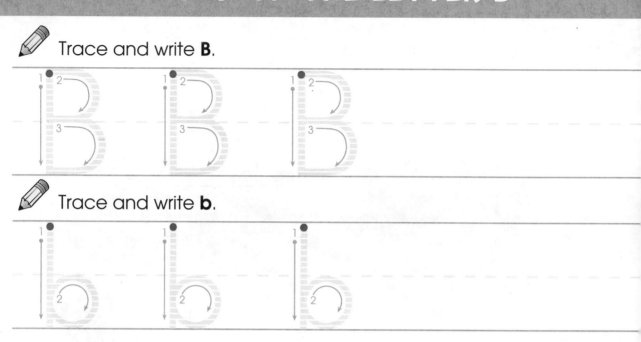

Trace and write **b**.

Color the picture.

Trace the letters to complete the sentence.

B is for boat.

the pictures that begin with **b**.

 Trace the missing **b** to finish each word.

bird   book

ball   baby

Trace and write **C**.

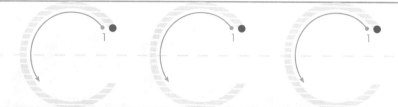

 Trace and write **c**.

 Color the picture.

 Trace the letters to complete the sentence.

C is for cow.

the pictures that begin with **c**.

 Trace the missing **c** to finish each word.

cat cake

coat cab

Trace and write each letter.

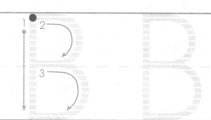

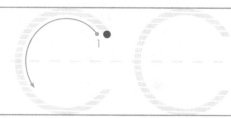

 Circle the letter that begins each picture word.

A B C

A B C

A B C

A B C

A B C

A B C

Trace and write each letter.

 a

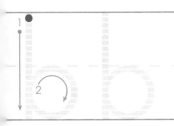 b b

c c

 Write the letter that begins the picture word. a b c

 nt

 upcake

 all

Trace and write **D**.

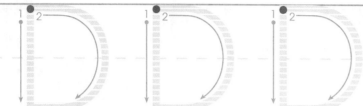

 Trace and write **d**.

 Color the picture.

 Trace the letters to complete the sentence.

D is for dog.

the pictures that begin with **d**.

 Trace the missing **d** to finish each word.

doll

drum

dad

duck

Trace and write **E**.

 Trace and write **e**.

 Color the picture.

 Trace the letters to complete the sentence.

E is for elephant

the pictures that begin with **e**.

 Trace the missing **e** to finish each word.

eggs eight **8**

elephant

Trace and write **F**.

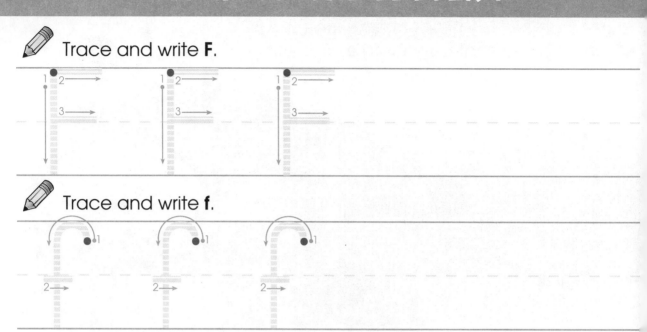

Trace and write **f**.

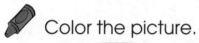

Color the picture.

Trace the letters to complete the sentence.

F is for fish.

the pictures that begin with **f**.

 Trace the missing **f** to finish each word.

an   ish

oot   rog

23

Trace and write each letter.

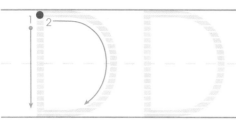

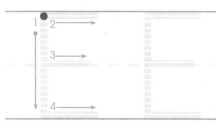

 Circle the letter that begins each picture word.

D E F

D E F

D E F

D E F

D E F

D E F

Trace and write each letter.

 d d

 e e

 f f

 Write the letter that begins the picture word. d e f

 oot

 gg

 og

Trace and write **G**.

 Trace and write **g**.

 Color the picture.

 Trace the letters to complete the sentence.

G is for girl.

the pictures that begin with **g**.

 Trace the missing **g** to finish each word.

goat   gift

girl   grapes

Trace and write **H**.

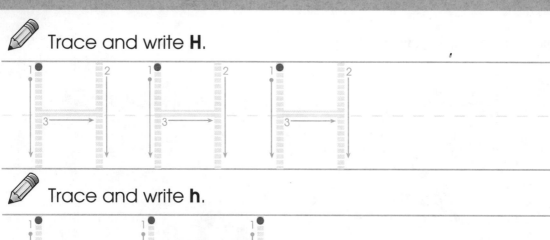

Trace and write **h**.

Color the picture.

Trace the letters to complete the sentence.

H is for hat.

the pictures that begin with **h**.

 Trace the missing **h** to finish each word.

horse   hat

hay   hook

Trace and write **I**.

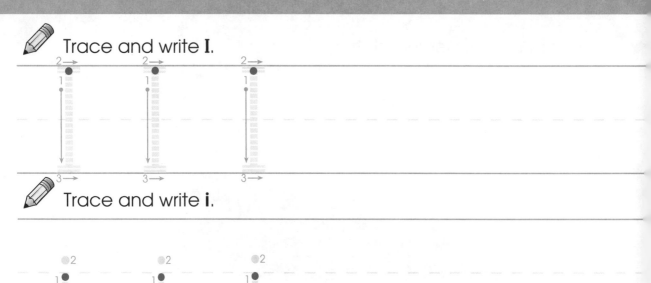

Trace and write **i**.

Color the picture.

Trace the letters to complete the sentence.

I is for iguana.

the pictures that begin with **i**.

 Trace the missing **i** to finish each word.

nk

nsect

gloo

vy

Trace and write each letter.

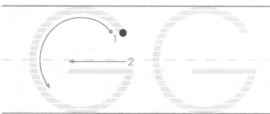

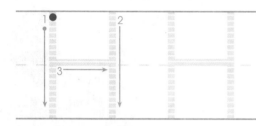

 Circle the letter that begins each picture word.

G   H   I

G   H   I

G   H   I

G   H   I

G   H   I

G   H   I

Trace and write each letter.

g g

h h

i i

 Write the letter that begins the picture word. g h i

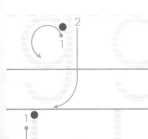 nsect

 at

 irl

Trace and write **J**.

Trace and write **j**.

Color the picture.

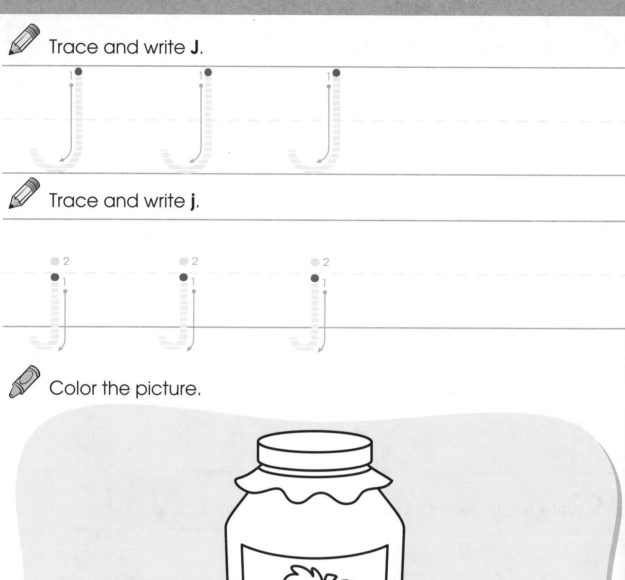

Trace the letters to complete the sentence.

J is for jelly.

the pictures that begin with **j**.

 Trace the missing **j** to finish each word.

jet jacks

jeans jar

Trace and write **K**.

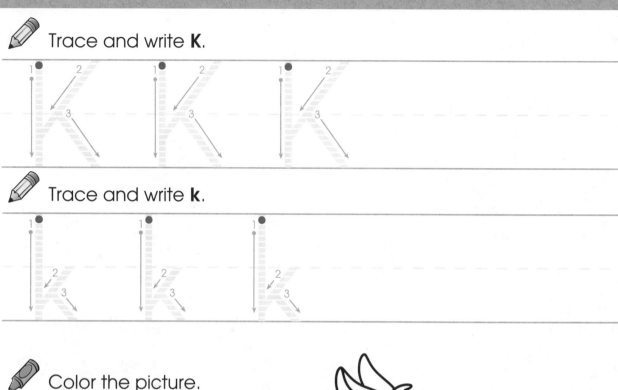

Trace and write **k**.

Color the picture.

Trace the letters to complete the sentence.

K is for kangaroo

the pictures that begin with **k**.

 Trace the missing **k** to finish each word.

kite

king

key

kitten

Trace and write **L**.

Trace and write **I**.

Color the picture.

Trace the letters to complete the sentence.

L is for lion.

the pictures that begin with **l**.

 Trace the missing **l** to finish each word.

amp

ion

ock

eaf

 Trace and write each letter.

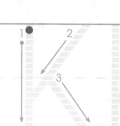

 Circle the letter that begins each picture word.

J K L

J K L

J K L

J K L

J K L

J K L

Trace and write each letter.

 Write the letter that begins the picture word. **j k l**

 et

 ey

 amp

Trace and write **M**.

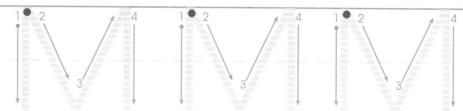

 Trace and write **m**.

 Color the picture.

 Trace the letters to complete the sentence.

M is for monkey.

the pictures that begin with **m**.

 Trace the missing **m** to finish each word.

mop

mouse

moon

milk

Trace and write **N**.

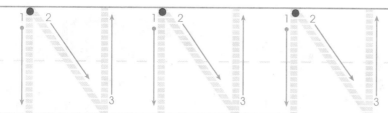

 Trace and write **n**.

 Color the picture.

 Trace the letters to complete the sentence.

N is for nuts.

the pictures that begin with **n**.

 Trace the missing **n** to finish each word.

nest

nail

net

nine

Trace and write **O**.

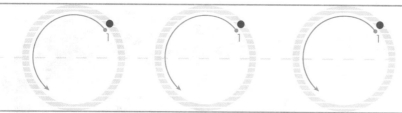

 Trace and write **o**.

 Color the picture.

 Trace the letters to complete the sentence.

O is for octopus.

the pictures that begin with **o**.

 Trace the missing **o** to finish each word.

owl

orange

onion

oven

Trace and write each letter.

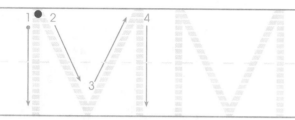

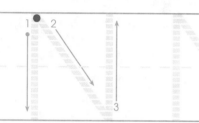

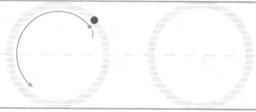

 Circle the letter that begins each picture word.

M N O

M N O

M N O

M N O

M N O

M N O

Trace and write each letter.

 m

 n

 o

 Write the letter that begins the picture word. **m n o**

 _____ ouse

 _____ est

 _____ x

✏️ Trace and write **P**.

P P P P P P

✏️ Trace and write **p**.

p p p p p p

🖍️ Color the picture.

✏️ Trace the letters to complete the sentence.

P is for pig.

the pictures that begin with **p**.

 Trace the missing **p** to finish each word.

pie

pizza

pear

pail

Trace and write **Q**.

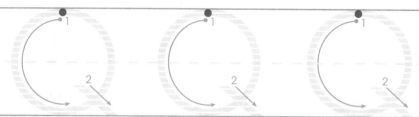

 Trace and write **q**.

 Color the picture.

 Trace the letters to complete the sentence.

Q is for queen.

the pictures that begin with **q**.

 Trace the missing **q** to finish each word.

quill   quilt

quail   quarter

Trace and write **R**.

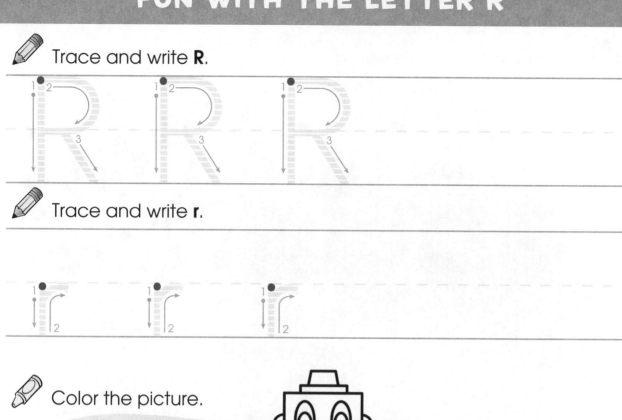

Trace and write **r**.

Color the picture.

Trace the letters to complete the sentence.

R is for robot.

the pictures that begin with **r**.

 Trace the missing **r** to finish each word.

ing

abbit

ope

ain

Trace and write each letter.

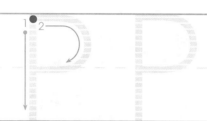

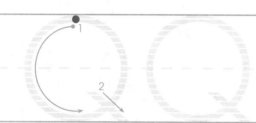

 Circle the letter that begins each picture word.

P   Q   R

P   Q   R

P   Q   R

P   Q   R

P   Q   R

P   Q   R

Trace and write each letter.

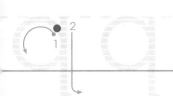

 Write the letter that begins the picture word. **p q r**

 ig

 ueen

 ing

Trace and write **S**.

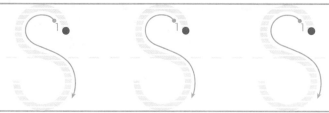

 Trace and write **s**.

 Color the picture.

 Trace the letters to complete the sentence.

S is for seal.

the pictures that begin with **s**.

 Trace the missing **s** to finish each word.

sun   spider

snail   sock

Trace and write **T**.

Trace and write **t**.

Color the picture.

Trace the letters to complete the sentence.

T is for Turkey.

the pictures that begin with **t**.

 Trace the missing **t** to finish each word.

ent   ree

able   rain

✏️ Trace and write **U**.

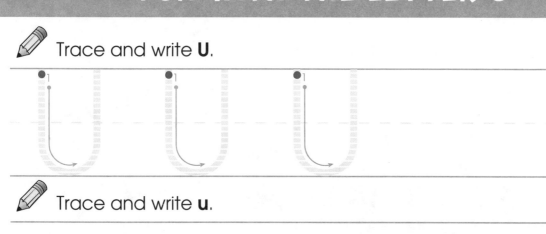

✏️ Trace and write **u**.

🖍️ Color the picture.

✏️ Trace the letters to complete the sentence.

U is for umpire.

the pictures that begin with **u**.

 Trace the missing **u** to finish each word.

up   under

umbrella

Trace and write each letter.

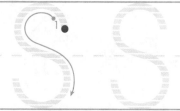

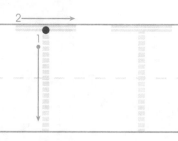

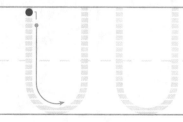

 Circle the letter that begins each picture word.

S T U

S T U

S T U

S T U

S T U

S T U

Trace and write each letter.

 Write the letter that begins the picture word. **s t u**

 un

  op

 p

Trace and write **V**.

 Trace and write **v**.

 Color the picture.

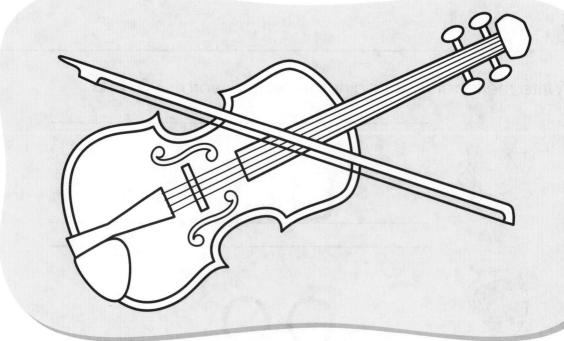

 Trace the letters to complete the sentence.

V is for violin.

the pictures that begin with **v**.

Trace the missing **v** to finish each word.

van   violin

vest   vase

Trace and write **W**.

 Trace and write **w**.

 Color the picture.

 Trace the letters to complete the sentence.

W is for whale.

the pictures that begin with **w**.

 Trace the missing **w** to finish each word.

web   worm

wagon   wolf

Trace and write **X**.

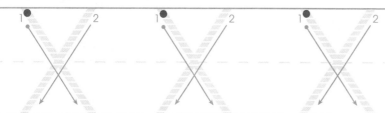

 Trace and write **x**.

 Color the picture.

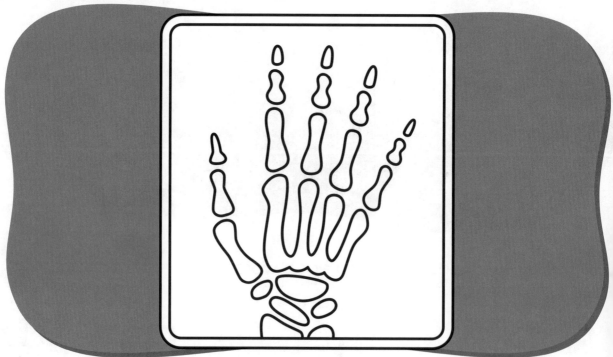

 Trace the letters to complete the sentence.

X is for x-ray.

✓ the **x**'s in the picture.

🖍 Color the **x**.

X

✏️ Trace and write **Xx**.

Trace and write each letter.

 Circle the letter that begins each picture word.

V   W   X

V   W   X

V   W   X

V   W   X

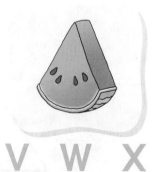

V   W   X

V   W   X

Trace and write each letter.

 Write the letter that begins the picture word. **V W X**

 ase

  orm

 -ray

73 Reviewing the Letters V, W & X

Trace and write **Y**.

 Trace and write **y**.

 Color the picture.

Trace the letters to complete the sentence.

Y is for yak.

the pictures that begin with **y**.

 Trace the missing **y** to finish each word.

yarn   yawn

yellow   yak

Trace and write **Z**.

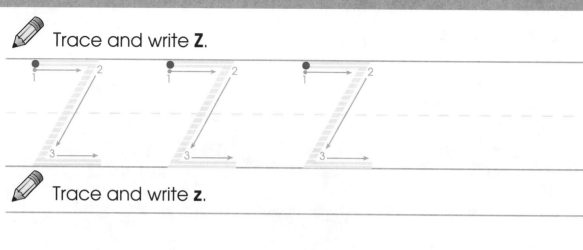

Trace and write **z**.

Color the picture.

Trace the letters to complete the sentence.

Z is for zebra.

the pictures that begin with **z**.

 Trace the missing **z** to finish each word.

zipper 　zero

zebra 　zoo

Trace and write each letter.

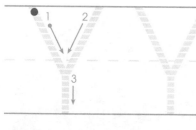

 Circle the letter that begins each picture word.

Y Z

Y Z

Y Z

Y Z

Trace and write each letter.

 Write the letter that begins the picture word. **y z**

 arn

 ipper

 oo

 o-yo

Trace the letters.
Write the missing letters.

Practicing Alphabetical Order

SHAPES & MEASUREMENT

This section is divided into two parts. The first portion focuses on learning to recognize and identify basic shapes. The second portion focuses on learning to describe and compare measurable attributes.

- The shape portion supplies a variety of activities that introduce the name and characteristics of a circle, square, triangle, and rectangle.

- For the kindergarten level, the measurement activities are simple comparisons of length, weight, and area. Practicing simple comparisons in this portion will help your child make the transition to standard measurements as his or her curriculum progresses.

Trace each shape.

Color the ☐ **purple**.

Color the ○ blue.

Color the △ green.

Color the ▭ orange.

rectangle   square   circle   triangle

A **circle** is a **shape** that looks like this: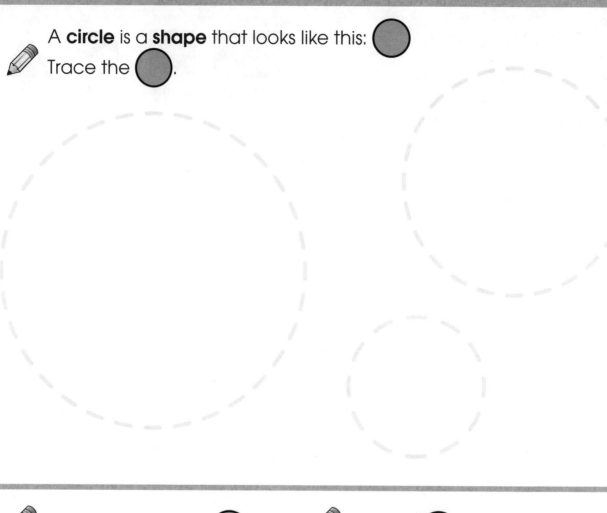

Trace the ◯.

 Make the shape a . Draw a .

✔ all of the ⬤ in the picture.

ow many ⬤ did you find?

_____

_____

A **square** is a **shape** that looks like this:

Trace the ☐ .

Make the shape a ☐ .   Draw a ☐ .

all of the  in the picture.

ow many ▢ did you find?

A **triangle** is a **shape** that looks like this:

Trace the .

 Make the shape a .   Draw a  .

88

all of the ▲ in the picture.

ow many ▲ did you find? _____

A **rectangle** is a **shape** that looks like this:

Trace the ⬚.

Make the shape a ⬚.   Draw a ⬚.

all of the ☐ in the picture.

ow many ☐ did you find? _____

SHAPE PATTERNS

 Draw and color the shape that comes next.

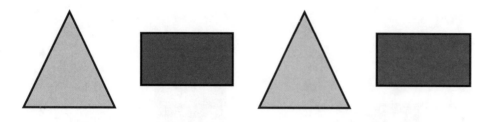

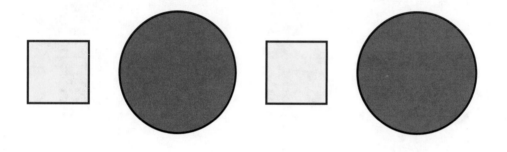

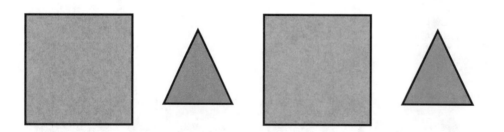

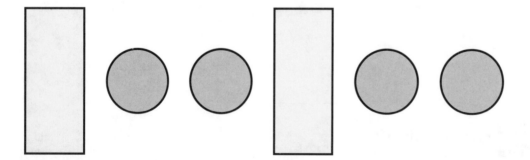

Trace each shape.
Find a shape in each picture that matches one of the shapes
you traced.
 Draw lines from the pictures to the shapes.

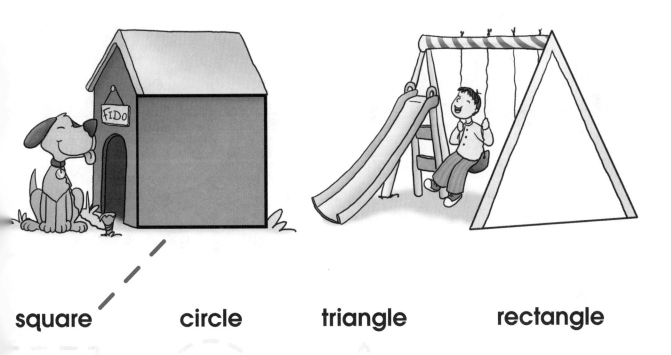

square   **circle**   **triangle**   **rectangle**

 Write how many of each shape:

Count the shapes.

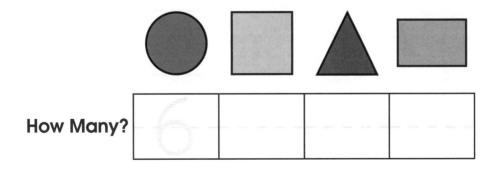

How Many? | 6 | | | |

✏️ Write how many of each shape:

◯ _____

▭ _____

◻ _____

△ _____

Count each shape.

How Many?

Color each ⬛ blue.

Color each 🔺 red.

Color each ⚪ yellow.

Color each ▬ green.

Write how many of each shape:

DRAW SHAPES

Connect dots to draw shapes.

square **rectangle** **triangle**

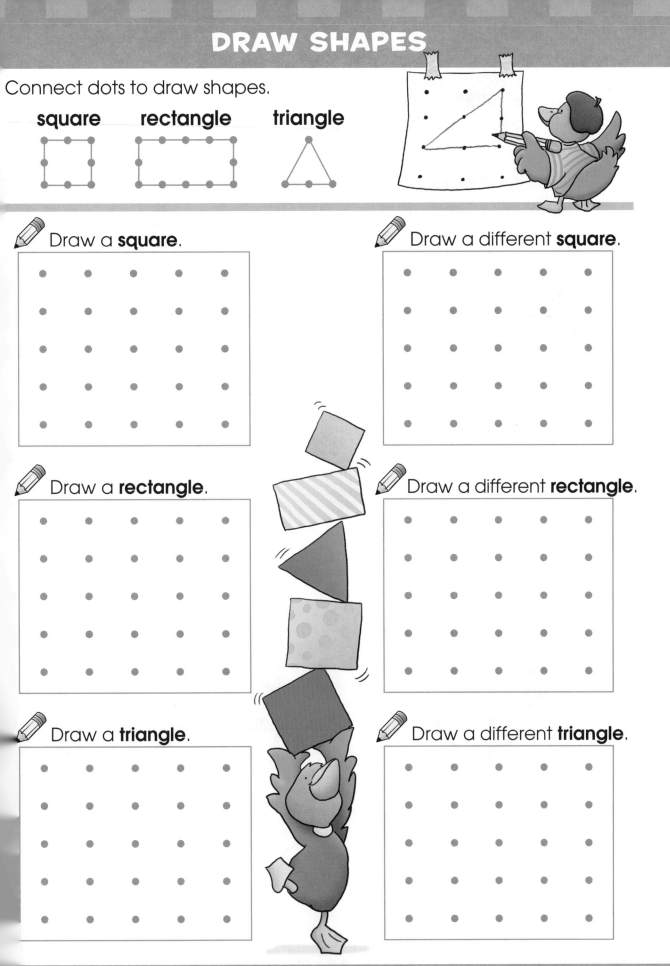

Draw a **square**.

Draw a different **square**.

Draw a **rectangle**.

Draw a different **rectangle**.

Draw a **triangle**.

Draw a different **triangle**.

Trace the **sides** of each shape.
Write how many **sides** each shape has.

____ **sides**

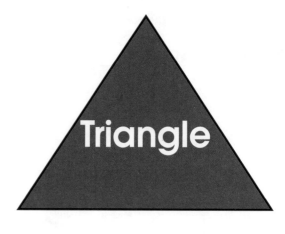

____ **sides**

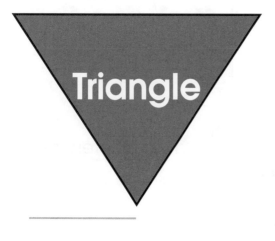

____ **sides**

____ **sides**

Circle the **corners** on each shape.
Write how many **corners** each shape has.

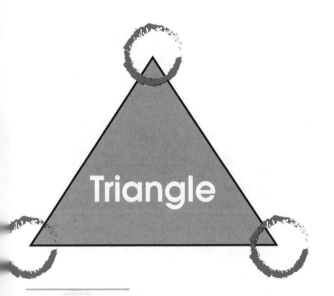

3 **corners**

_____ **corners**

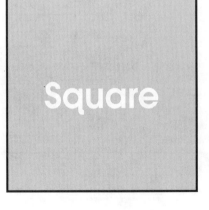

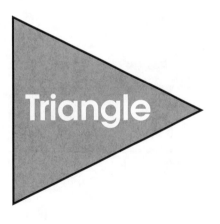

_____ **corners**

_____ **corners**

A **cube** is a **shape** that looks like this:

How many can you find? _____

_____

_____

A **sphere** is a **shape** that looks like this:

How many can you find? _____

THE CONE

A **cone** is a **shape** that looks like this:

How many can you find? _____

A **cylinder** is a **shape** that looks like this:

How many can you find? _____

Draw lines from the objects to the matching figures.

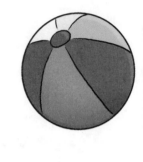

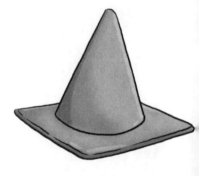

3-D PATTERNS

 Circle the shape that comes next.

    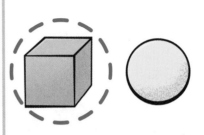

   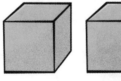

COMPARING SIZE

Circle the **shorter** picture in each group.
✗ the **taller** picture in each group.

COMPARING VOLUME

Circle the picture that holds **more**.

COMPARING WEIGHT

 Circle which is **heavier**.

 Circle which is **lighter**.

Circle the **lighter** objects.

Draw lines to match the flowers to the correct pots.
Use a different color for each line.

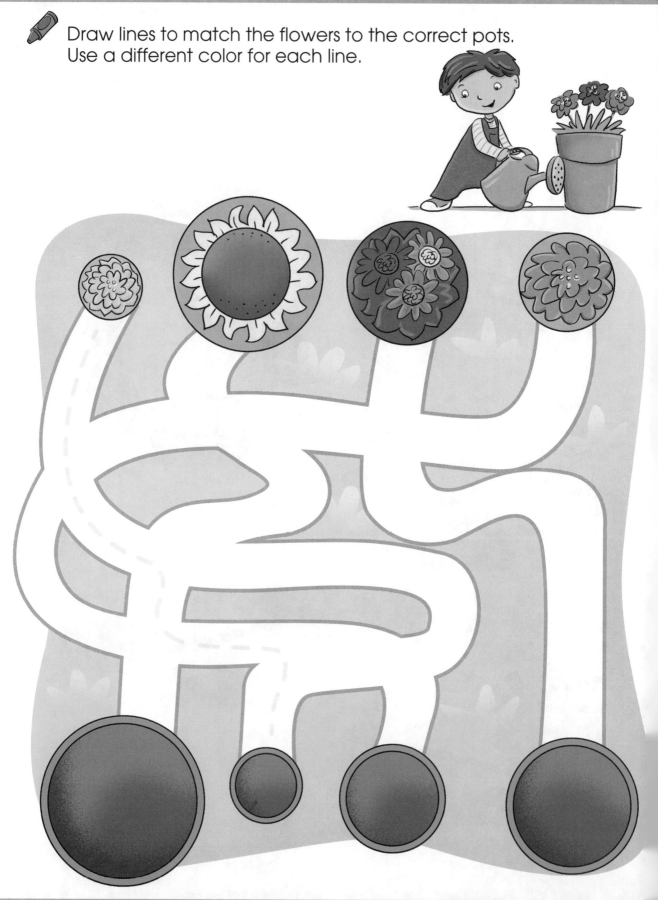

NUMBERS 0-20

This section will help your child develop some important early math skills, including: recognizing the numbers 0–20, counting, relating numerals to number words, writing numerals and number words, and matching numbers to groups of objects. Here are some tips to help your child get the most from this section:

- To help your child learn the numbers in numerical order, encourage your child to work from the beginning to the end of this section.

- The pages have both number words and numerals to ensure that your child will learn to recognize both. Encourage your child to say each number and count the symbols that show each amount.

- The writing component will help your child practice writing both numerals and number words. The pages show the proper starting points for each stroke. Encourage your child to follow the arrows, which will help your child form the numerals and number words correctly.

- After your child has completed the activities in this section, encourage him or her to practice what he or she has learned by making groups of various amounts with objects you have around the house.

This basket has **0** puppies in it.

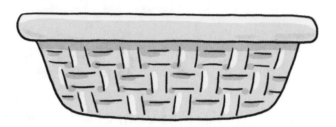

 Trace and write the number **0**.

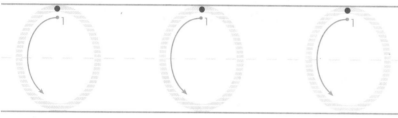

Circle the puppies that have **0** spots.

Circle the baskets that have **0** puppies inside.

 Trace and write **zero**.

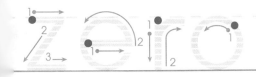

I
one

Count I

 Trace and write the number I.

 Circle the groups that have I animal.

Color 1  **red**.

 Color 1 🦃 **brown**.

How many 🐄?

 Trace and write **one**.

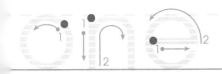

2
two

Count 2

Trace and write the number **2**.

Color **2** 🐕 **brown**.

Draw **2** ⊗ on the 😀.

How many 🐤?

_____

_____

Trace and write **two**.

t w o

3
three

Count 3 .

 Trace and write the number **3**.

 Circle the groups of **3**.

Color **3**  orange.

Color **3** 🐥 yellow.

How many ☁️?.

_____

_____

_____

Trace and write **three**.

three

4
four

Count 4 .

 Trace and write the number **4**.

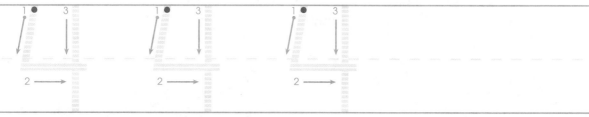

Circle the groups of **4**.

Color **4** 🖍️ purple.

Color **4** 🎃 orange.

How many 🐐 ?

_____

_____

_____

✏️ Trace and write **four**.

5
five

Count 5 .

 Trace and write the number **5**.

 Circle the groups of **5**.

Color **5** 🌷 **purple**.

Color **5** 🍎 **red**.

How many 🐰?

_____

_____

_____

Trace and write **five**.

 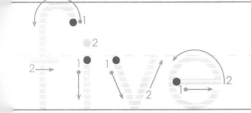

Connect the dots from **1** to **5**.
Color the picture.

COUNT, COLOR & WRITE

Count　　　🖍 **Color**　　　✏️ **Write**

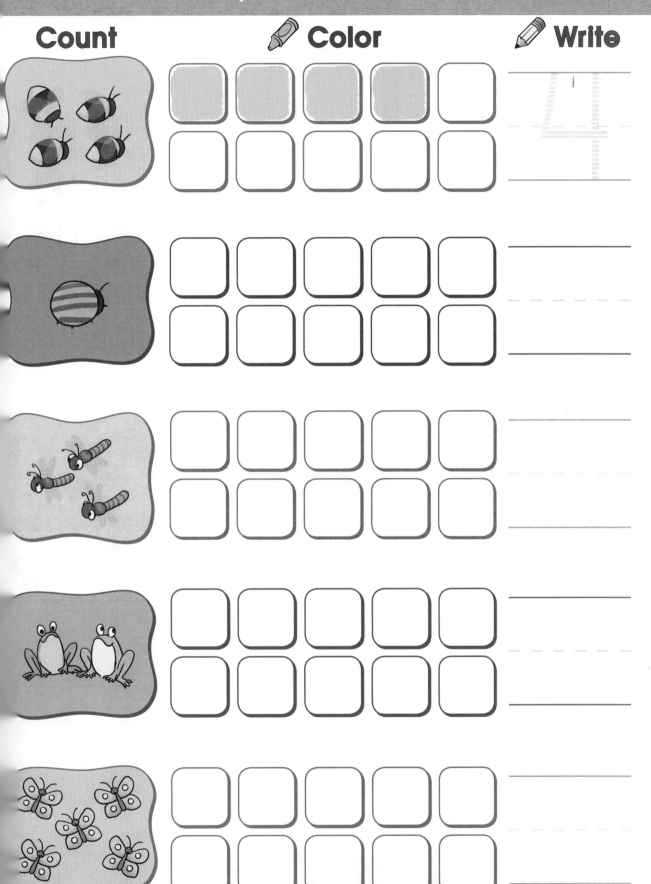

Draw a line from each number to the correct group.
Write each number by the correct group.

1

3

_____

2

5

4

_____

_____

COUNT & COLOR

Count.
Color to match the number.

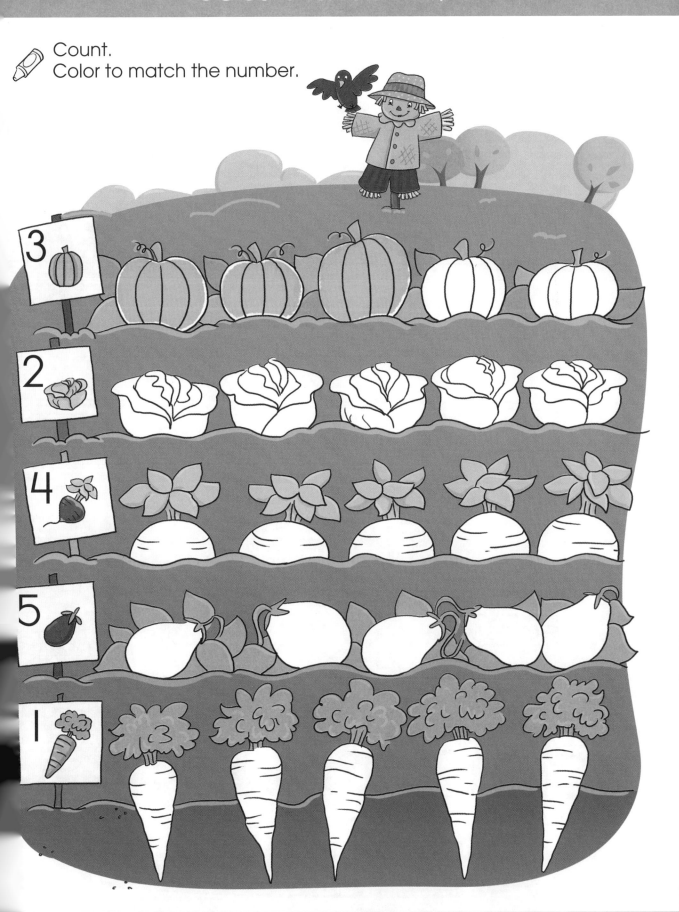

6
six

Count 6

✏️ Trace and write the number **6**.

6 6 6

✏️ Circle the groups of **6**.

Color **6** green.

Color **6** ◯ brown.

How many ?

_____

_____

Trace and write **six**.

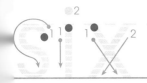

7
seven

Count **7** .

 Trace and write the number **7**.

 Circle the groups of **7**.

Color **7**  orange.

Draw **7** on the .

How many ?

_____

_____

_____

Trace and write **seven**.

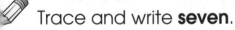

8

eight

Count **8** 🍎.

 Trace and write the number **8**.

 Circle the groups of **8**.

Color **8** **red**.

 Color **8** 🍃 **green**.

How many 🐤?

_____

_____

_____

 Trace and write **eight**.

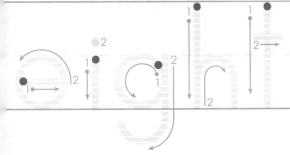

9 nine

Count 9 .

 Trace and write the number **9**.

Circle the groups of **9**.

Color **9** brown.

 Color **1** green to make **9**.

How many ?

_____

_____

_____

 Trace and write **nine**.

FUN WITH THE NUMBER TEN

10 ten

Count 10 .

Trace and write the number 10.

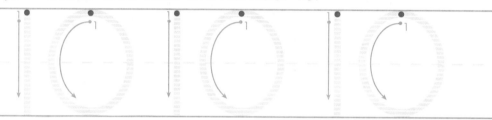

Circle the groups of 10.

Color **10** 🐟.

 Draw **10** ⭐.

How many  ?

_____

- - - - - - - - -

_____

 Trace and write **ten**.

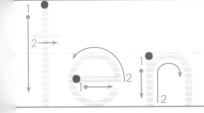

Connect the dots from **0** to **10**.
Color the picture.

COUNT, COLOR & WRITE

Count	Color	Write

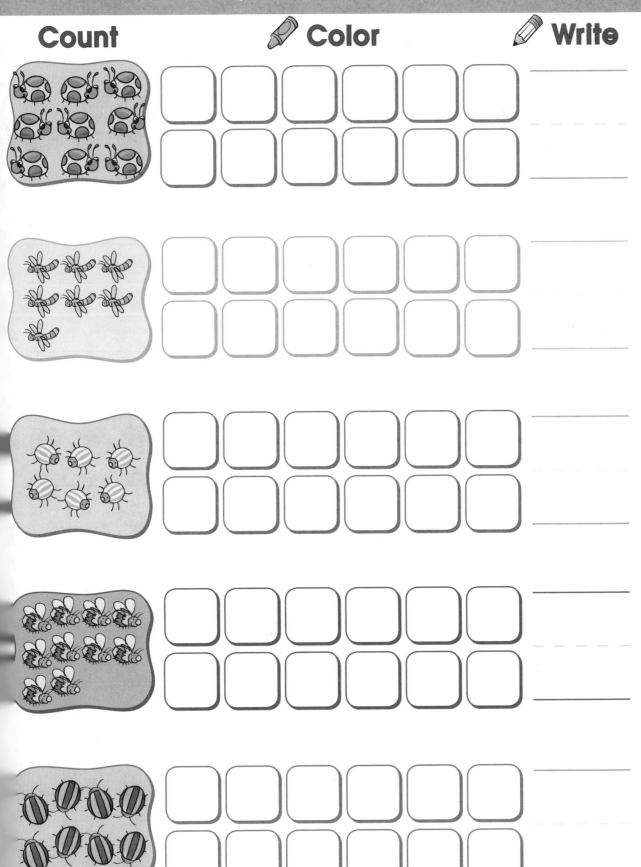

Draw a line from each number to the correct group.
Write each number by the correct group.

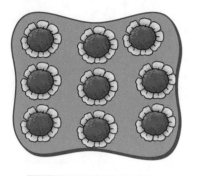

7

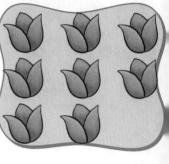

10

6

9

8

Count.
Color to match the number.

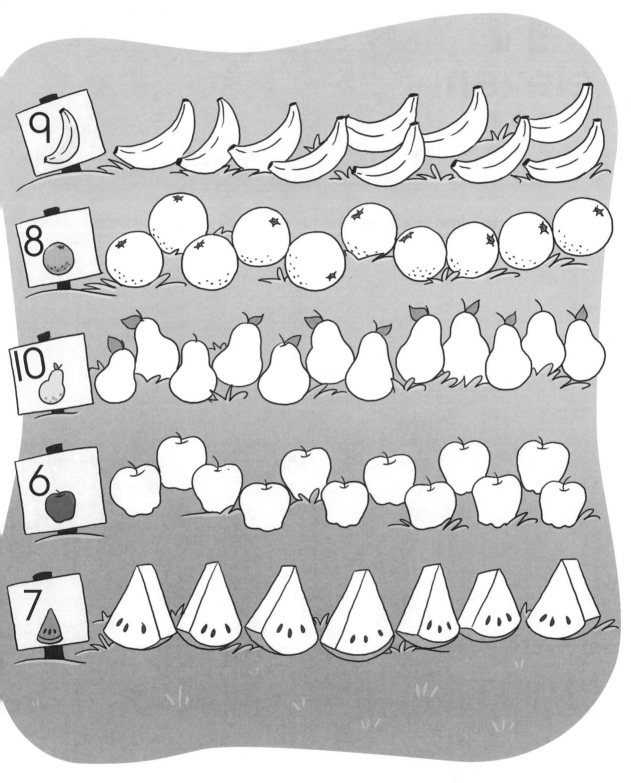

FUN WITH THE NUMBER ELEVEN

11
eleven

Count 11.

 Trace and write the number 11.

 Circle the groups of 11.

Color **11** △.

 Draw **11** ⌒.

How many 🏠?

_____

_____

_____

 Trace **eleven**.

12
twelve

Count 12 .

 Trace and write the number 12.

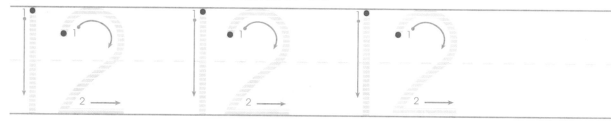

 Circle the groups of 12.

Follow the path of **12**s to help the
sailor get to the boat.

How many 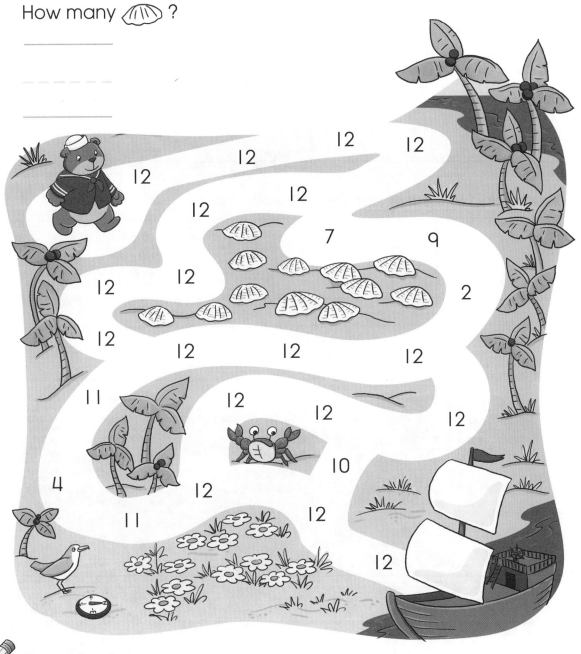 ?

_____

_____

_____

Trace **twelve**.

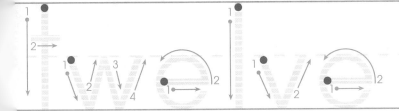

Count 13 .

 Trace and write the number **13**.

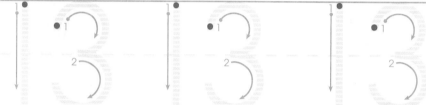

Which group has **13**?

Color **13** pink.

 13 ☆.

How many 🛸 ?

_____

_____

_____

 Trace **thirteen**.

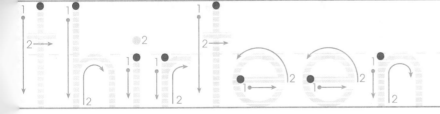

14
fourteen

Count 14 🌲.

✏️ Trace and write the number 14.

Which group has 14? 🧊 ❄️

Color **14** blue.

 14 .

How many ◉?

_____

_____

 Trace **fourteen**.

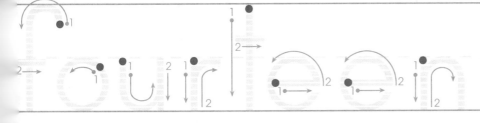

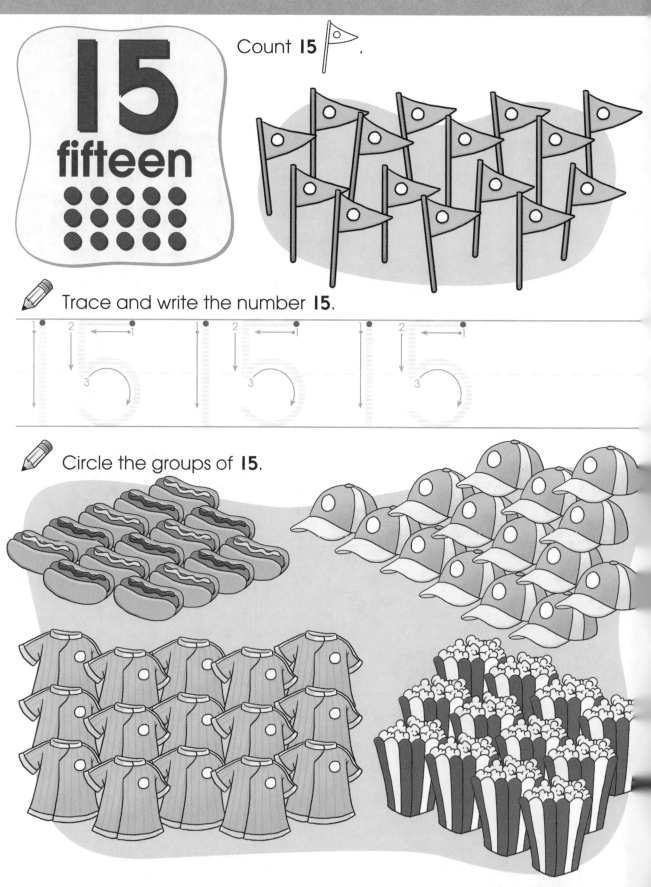

15

fifteen

Count 15 🚩.

Trace and write the number **15**.

Circle the groups of **15**.

Color **15** ◯ .

 15 .

How many 🖾 ?

_____

_____

_____

 Trace **fifteen**.

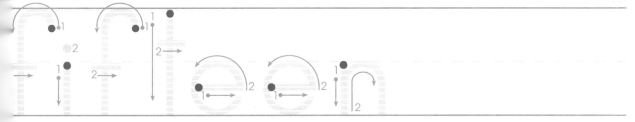

DOWN THE RIVER

Connect the dots from **1** to **15**.
Color the picture.

COUNT, COLOR & WRITE

Count　　　🖍 **Color**　　　✏️ **Write**

Draw a line from each number to the correct group.
Write each number by the correct group.

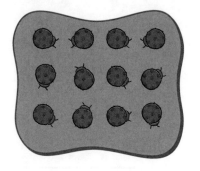

13

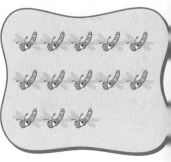

_____

___ ___ ___ ___

11

_____

_____

___ ___ ___ ___

14

_____

15

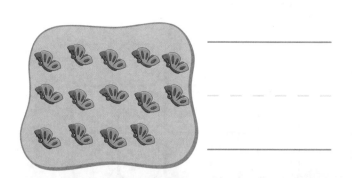

_____

___ ___ ___ ___

12

_____

_____

___ ___ ___ ___

COUNT & COLOR

Count.
Color to match the number.

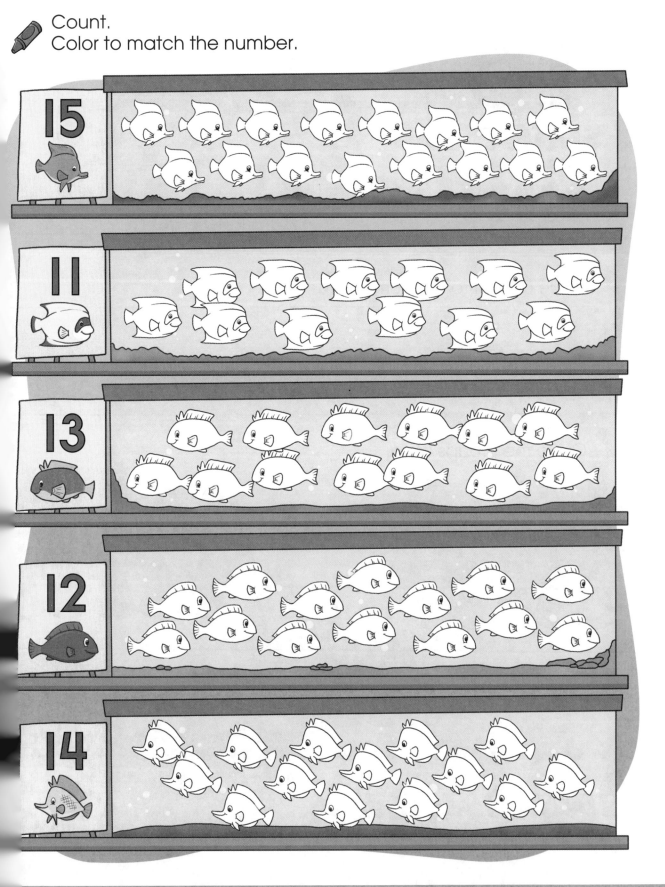

16
sixteen

Count 16 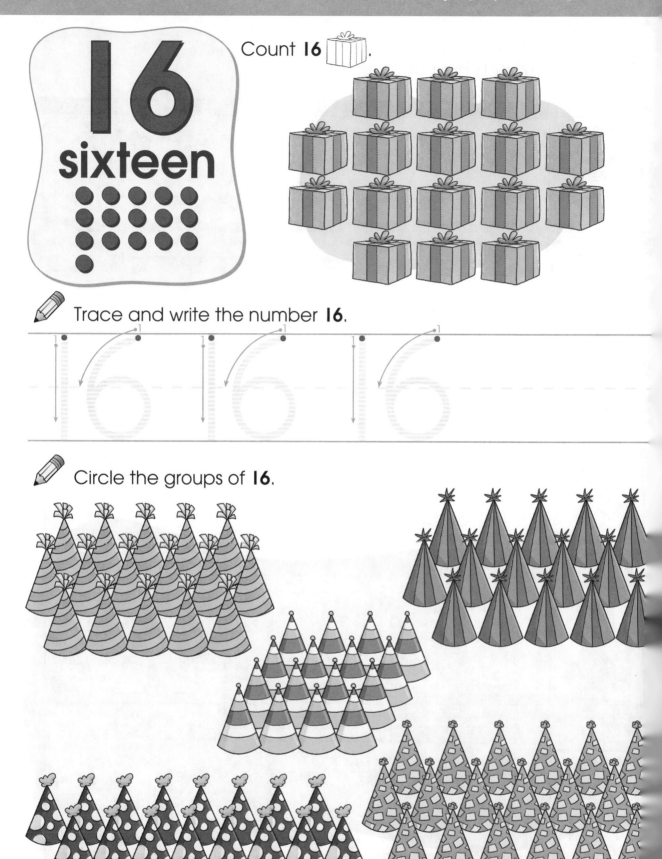.

Trace and write the number 16.

Circle the groups of 16.

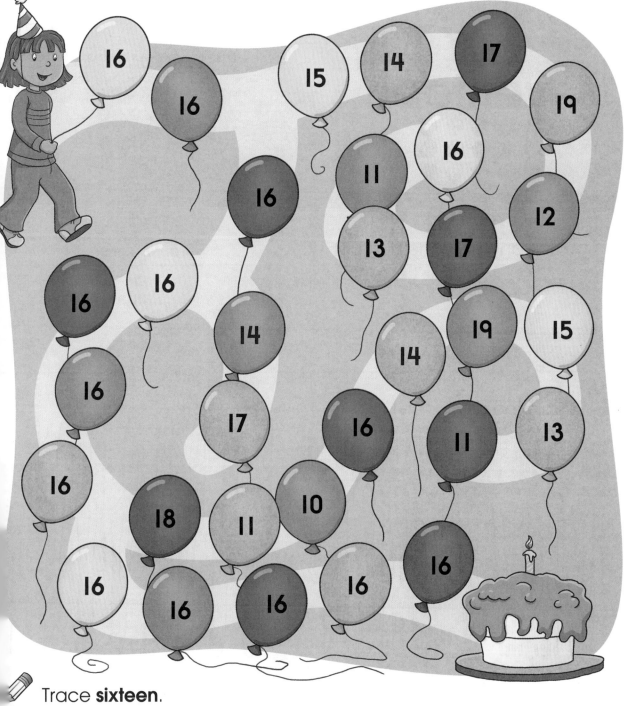

Trace **sixteen**.

sixteen

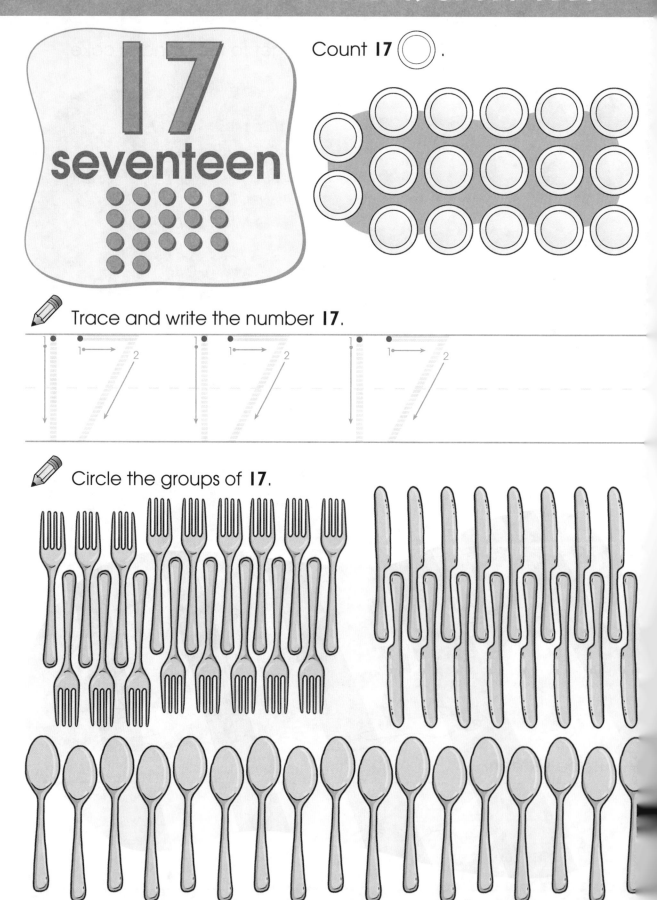

17
seventeen

Count 17 ◯ .

Trace and write the number **17**.

Circle the groups of **17**.

Color **17** **brown**.

 Color **17** orange.

How many 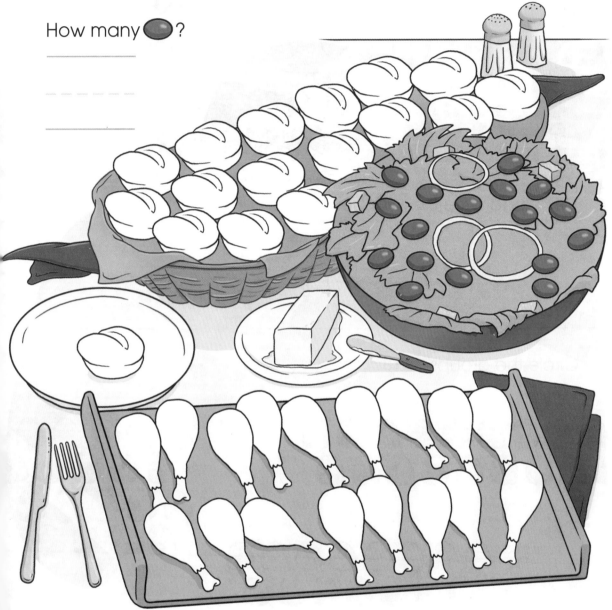?

_____

_____

 Trace **seventeen**.

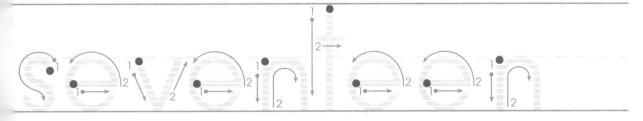

Count 18 .

 Trace and write the number **18**.

 Circle the groups of **18**.

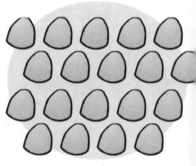

Color **18** ◯ **red**.

✓ **18** 🥤 .

How many 🍭 ?

_____

_____

_____

🖉 Trace **eighteen**.

eighteen

19
nineteen

Count 19 ✏.

Trace and write the number 19.

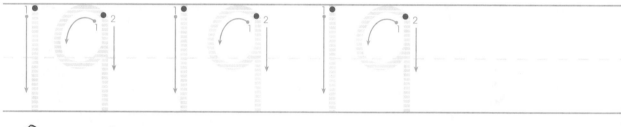

Circle the groups of 19.

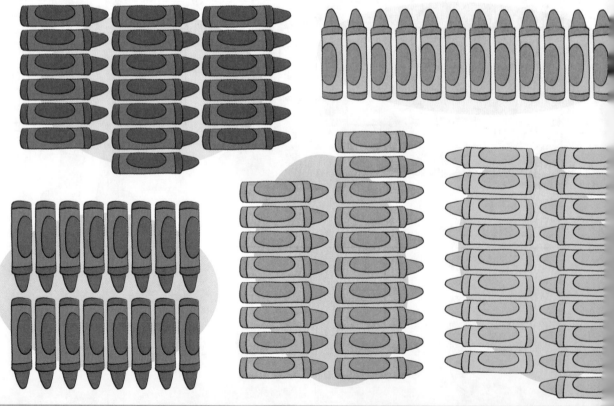

Color 19  purple.

19 🪣 .

How many 🐭 ?

_____

_____

Trace **nineteen**.

nineteen

Count **20** .

 Trace and write the number **20**.

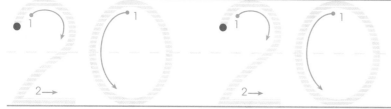

 Circle the groups of **20**.

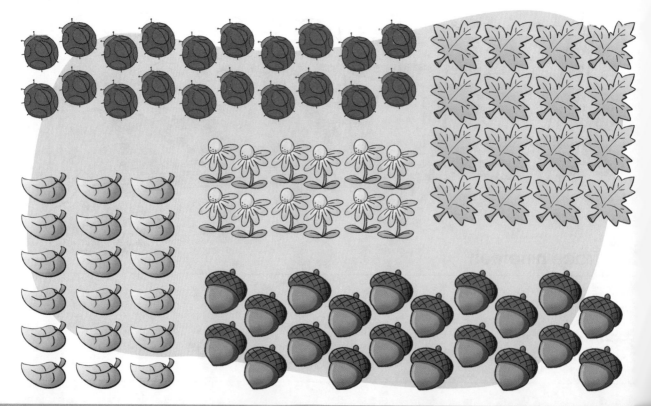

✏️ Trace the path from **1-20**.

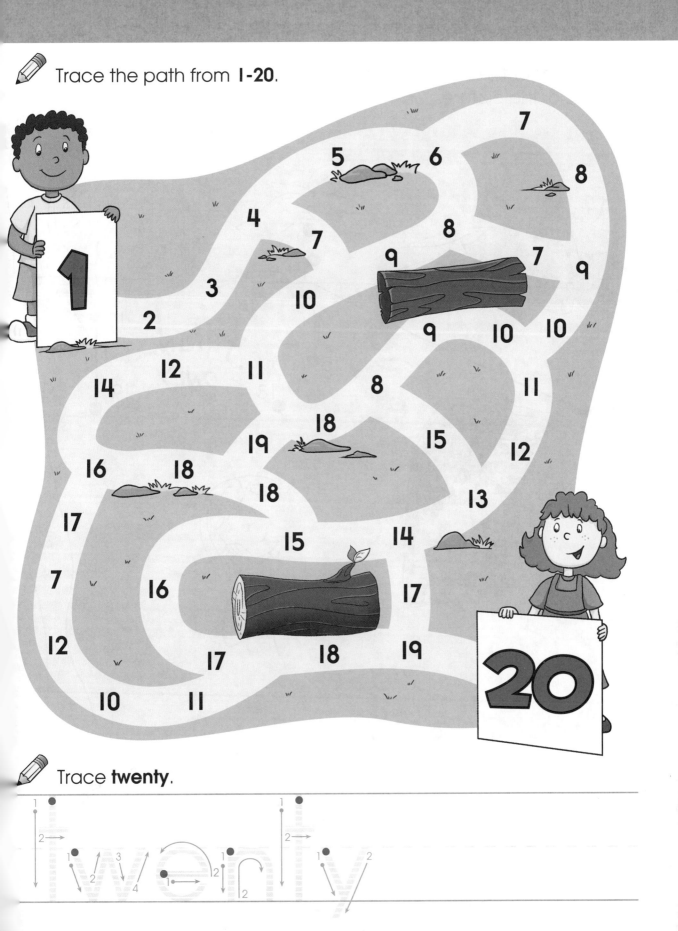

✏️ Trace **twenty**.

Connect the dots from **1** to **20**.
Color the picture.

COUNT, COLOR & WRITE

Count	Color	Write

_____

_ _ _ _ _ _ _ _ _

_____

NUMBER MATCHING

 Draw a line from each number to the correct group.
Write each number by the correct group.

_____

- - - - - - - - - -

_____

18

19

16

20

17

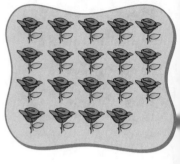

_____

- - - - - - - - - -

_____

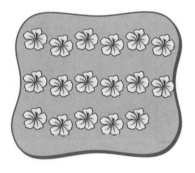

_____

- - - - - - - - - -

_____

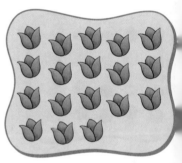

_____

- - - - - - - - - -

_____

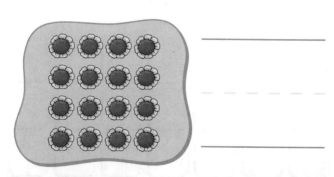

_____

- - - - - - - - - -

_____

COUNT & COLOR

Count.
Color to match the number.

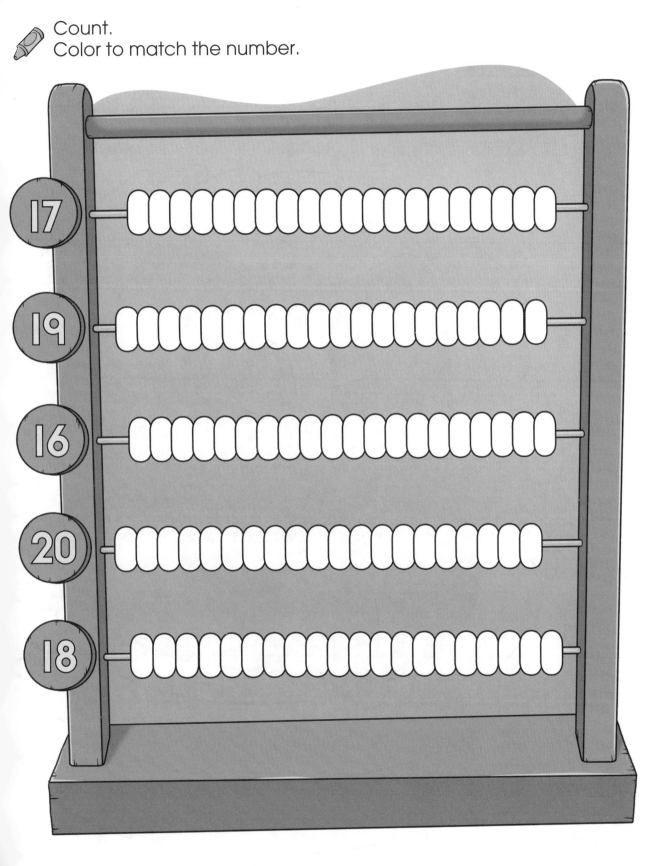

Color the picture.

2 = red
4 = yellow
6 = green
8 = blue
10 = orange
12 = black

A DAY AT THE POND

 Color the picture.

1 = red

3 = blue

5 = orange

7 = brown

9 = green

11 = yellow

TRANSITION MATH

This section contains math activities that will help your child get ready for first grade math. The interesting lessons focus on an assortment of the math skills needed for first grade, including: understanding numbers through 20, working with the concepts of more/greater and fewer/less, exploring the concepts of before, between, and after, identifying and extending patterns, working with tally marks, learning to add and subtract, working with graphs, telling time to the hour, counting amounts of money to 20 cents comprised of pennies, nickels, and dimes, and working with fractions. Since the lessons in this section build on concepts and skills taught in previous lessons, encourage your child to proceed from the beginning to the end of this section.

Trace and write the numbers.

zero

one

two

three

four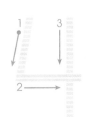

five

Draw a line from the group to the number.

0

1

2

3

4

5

COUNTING & WRITING NUMBERS

 Count.
Write the number in the box.

Trace and write the numbers.

six

seven

eight

nine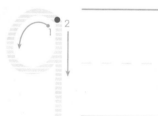

ten

COUNTING & MATCHING

✏️ Draw a line from the group to the number.

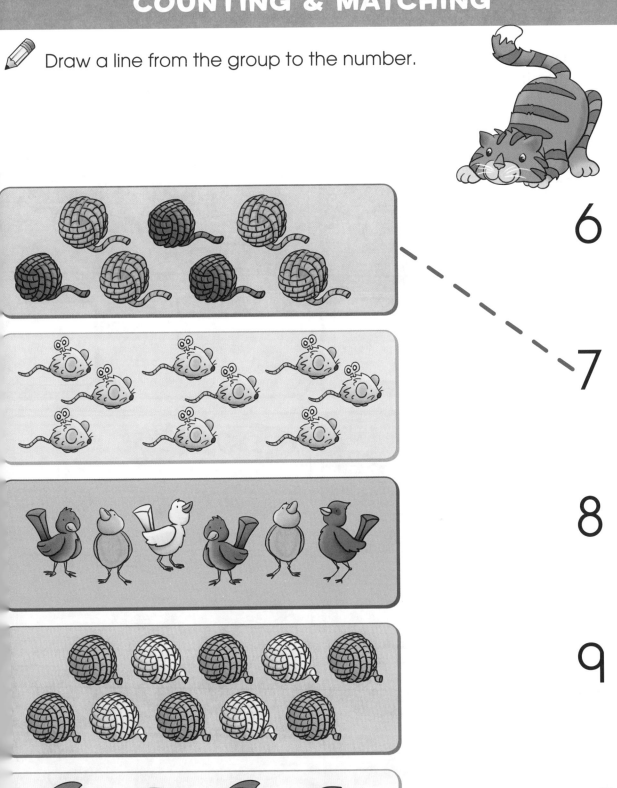

6

7

8

9

10

COUNTING & WRITING NUMBERS

 Count.
Write the number in the box.

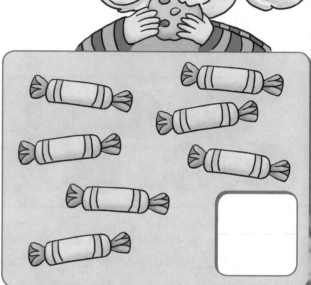

Read the number.
Color that number of objects.

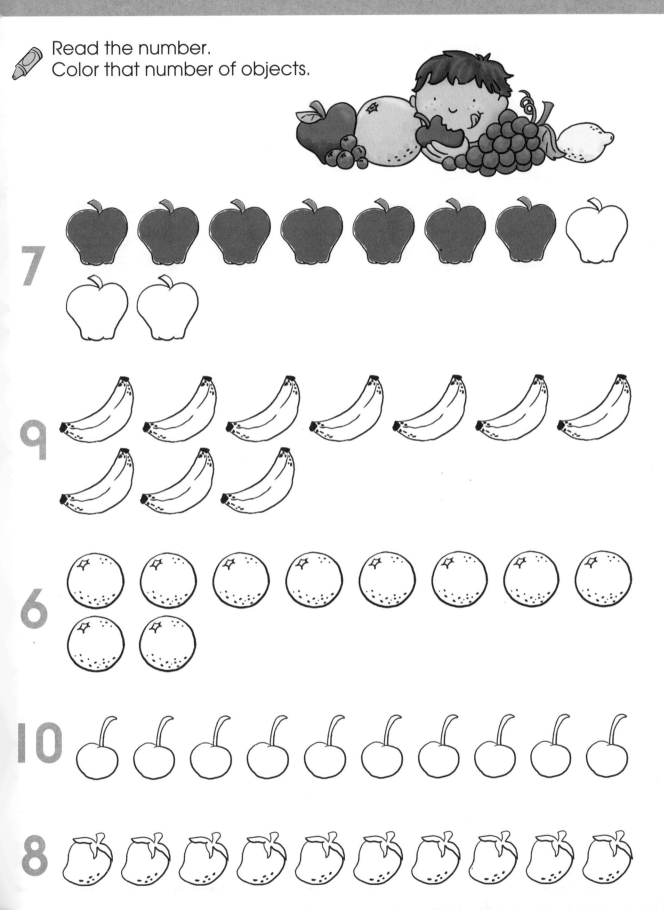

7

9

6

10

8

Write the missing numbers.

0 1 2 3 4 5 6 7 8 9 10 11 12

0 1 2 3 4 5 6

1 3 6

4 6 8

4 7 9

6 10

SAME NUMBER

How many are there? **③** **4** **5**

How many are there? **③** **4** **5**

 Draw to show the same number as .

How many are there? **4** **5** **6**

How many are there? **4** **5** **6**

Learning the Concept of *Same*

Which group has **more** objects?
Match the objects one to one.
Circle the number that is **greater**.

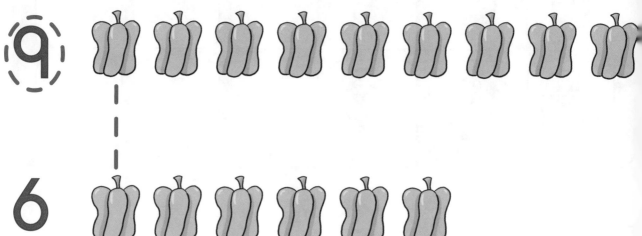

9
6

8
7

4
8

Count.
Write the number.
Circle the group that has **more**.

 5

  3

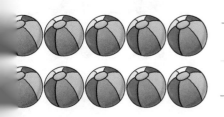

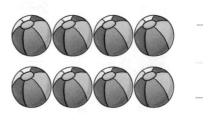

Count.
Circle the group that has **1 more**.

3

1

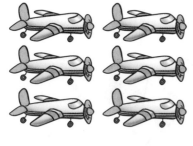

6

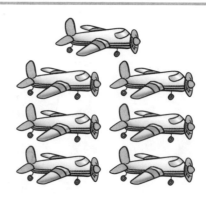

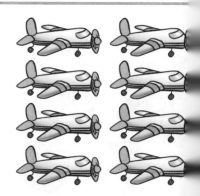

4

Count.
Circle the group that has **I more**.

I

3

2

5

Which group has **fewer** objects?
Match the objects one to one.
Circle the number that is **less**.

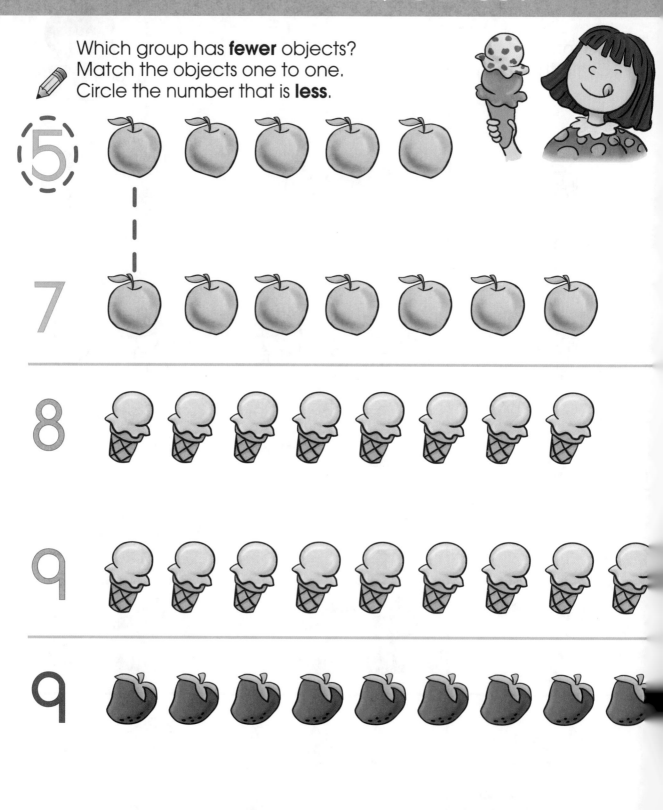

Count.
Write the number.
Circle the group that has **fewer**.

 4

 6

Count.
Circle the group that has **1 fewer**.

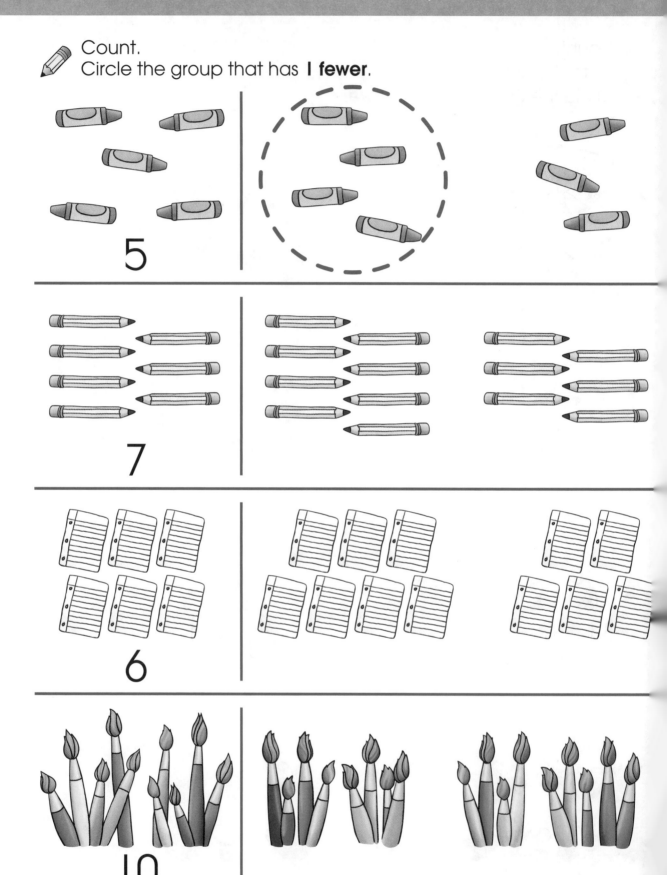

5

7

6

10

Count.
Circle the group that has **1 fewer**.

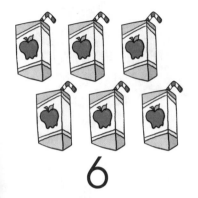

6

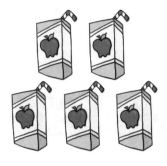

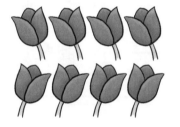

8

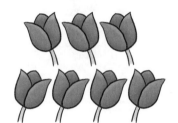

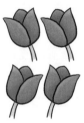

4

5

ww.anywhereteacher.com
191
Learning the Concept of *Fewer*

Write the missing numbers.

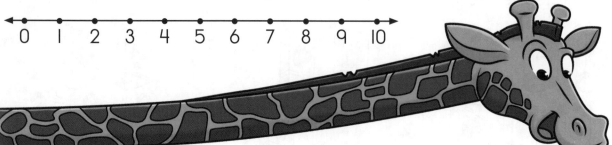

0 1 2 3 4 5 6 7 8 9 10

1 2 3 ___ 5

4 5 6 7 ___

6 7 8 9 ___

2 3 4 ___ 6

Which number comes before?

1 2 3

1 comes **before** 2.

✏️ Write the number that comes **before**.

_____ 3 4   _____ 7 8

_____ 5 6   _____ 9 10

_____ 8 9   _____ 6 7

Which number comes between?

1 2 3

2 comes **between** 1 and 3.

✏️ Write the number that comes **between**.

2 __ 4   5 __ 7

4 __ 6   7 __ 9

6 __ 8   8 __ 10

Which number comes after?

1 2 3

3 comes **after** 2.

✏️ Write the number that comes **after**.

2 3 ___   6 7 ___

7 8 ___   4 5 ___

8 9 ___   1 2 ___

Trace and write the numbers.

eleven

twelve

thirteen

fourteen

fifteen

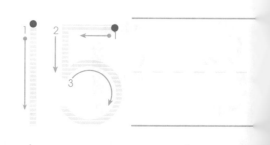

COUNTING & WRITING NUMBERS

 Count.
Write the number in the box.

WHICH NUMBER IS GREATER?

 Match the objects one to one.
Circle the number that is **greater**.

6

5

3

4

9

7

Count.
Write the number.
Circle the group that has **more**.

 _____

 _____

 _____

 _____

 _____

 _____

 _____

 _____

WHICH NUMBER IS LESS?

Match the objects one to one.
Circle the number that is **less**.

1

3

5

4

6

7

Practicing the Concept of *Less*   200   ©School Zone Publishing Compa

Count.
Write the number.
Circle the group that has **fewer**.

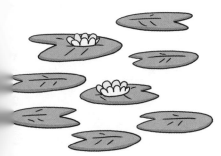 

Trace and write the numbers.

sixteen

seventeen

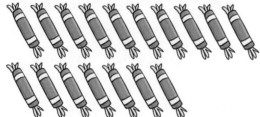

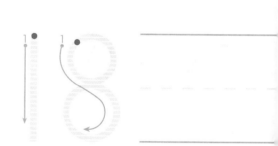

eighteen

nineteen

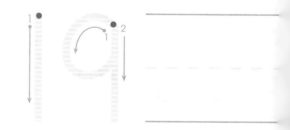

twenty

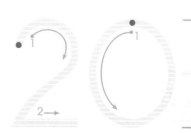

COUNT & WRITE

 Count.
Write the number in the box.

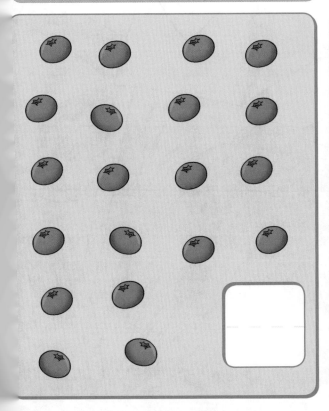

HIDDEN NUMBERS

 The numbers **5, 7, 8, 12, 13, 15, 16, 18,** and **20** are hidden in the picture.
Find and circle the numbers.

DRAWING MISSING OBJECTS

 Read the number.
Draw the missing objects to make the group of objects match the number.

12

15

11

17

20

12 comes **before** 13.

12 13 14

 Write the number that comes **before** these numbers.

_____ 17 18   _____ 19 20

_____ 14 15   _____ 10 11

_____ 18 19   _____ 16 17

BETWEEN

14 comes **between** 13 and 15.

13 14 15

 Write the number that comes **between** these numbers.

   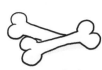

16 ___ 18   10 ___ 12

18 ___ 20   17 ___ 19

12 ___ 14   15 ___ 17

17 comes **after** 16.

15 16 **17**

✏️ Write the number that comes **after** these numbers.

13 14 ___

18 19 ___

17 18 ___

11 12 ___

10 11 ___

14 15 ___

✏️ Write the missing numbers.

5 _ _ _ _ _ _ 9 _

7 _ 9 _ _ _ _ _ 12

_ 4 _ _ 6 _ 8

13 _ _ _ 16 17 _

_ 16 _ _ _ 19 _

MORE

Count.
Write the number.
Circle the group that has **more** objects.

_____   _____

_____   _____

   _____      _____

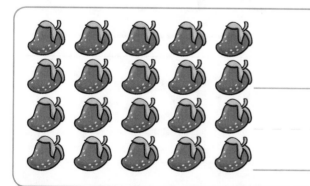   _____   _____

Read the numbers.
Draw that many Xs.
Circle the number that is **greater**.

13 X X X X X X X X X X
   X X X — — — — — — —

12 — — — — — — — — — —

7 — — — — — — — — — —

10 — — — — — — — — — —

15 — — — — — — — — — —

17 — — — — — — — — — —

9 — — — — — — — — — —

19 — — — — — — — — — —

FEWER

 Count.
Write the number.
Circle the group that has **fewer** objects.

 _____

 _____

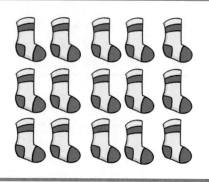 _____

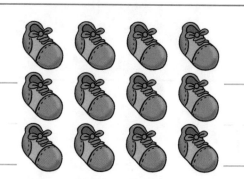 _____

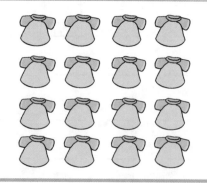 _____

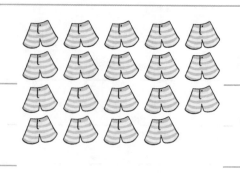 _____

 _____

Read the numbers.
Draw that many **X**s.
Circle the number that is **less**.

9 —————————————

6 —————————————

13 —————————————

15 —————————————

7 —————————————

17 —————————————

19 —————————————

14 —————————————

Color the window to complete each pattern.

CLOTHESLINE PATTERNS

 Color the one that comes next to complete each pattern.

Circle the object that comes next.

    |

    |

    |

   |

Copy the patterns.

Tally marks are used to count things.

| = one item

‖‖| = five items

 Draw tally marks for the numbers.

1   2   3   4   5

6   7   8   9   10

 Connect the dots from | to ‖‖ ‖‖.
Color the picture.

TALLY MARKS

✏️ Count each animal using tally marks.
✏️ Then write each number.

||||

Adding shows **how many there are in all**.

 Count.
Write how many there are in all.

$1 + 1 = 2$

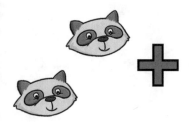

$2 + 0 = 2$

$3 + 0 = 3$

$1 + 2 = 2$

Count.
Write how many there are in all.

$2 + 2 = 4$

$3 + 1 = 4$

$1 + 3 = 4$

$0 + 4 = 4$

Count.
Write how many there are in all.

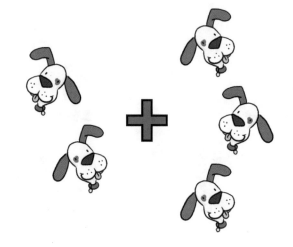

$1 + 4 = 5$

$2 + 3 = 5$

$5 + 0 = 5$

$3 + 2 = 5$

Count.
Write how many there are in all.

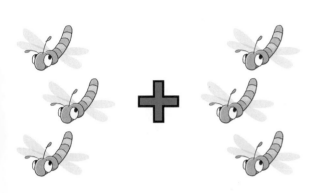

$3 + 3 = 6$

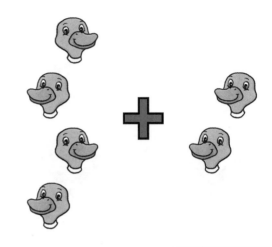

$4 + 2 = 6$

$5 + 1 = 6$

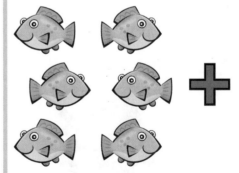

$6 + 0 = 6$

Subtracting shows **how many are left**.

 Count.
Write how many are left.

$$5 - 4 = \underline{\qquad}$$

$$1 - 0 = \underline{\qquad}$$

$$2 - 1 = \underline{\qquad}$$

$$3 - 2 = \underline{\qquad}$$

Count.
Write how many are left.

4 - 2 = _____

3 - 1 = _____

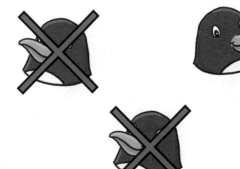

5 - 3 = _____

2 - 0 = _____

Count.
Write how many are left.

$4 - 1 =$ _____

$3 - 0 =$ _____

$5 - 2 =$ _____

$6 - 3 =$ _____

Count.
Write how many are left.

5 - 1 =

6 - 2 =

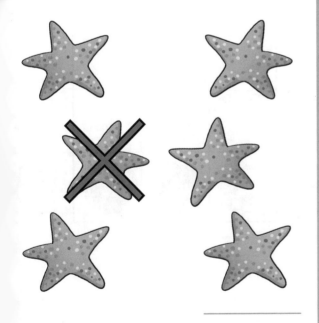

6 - 1 =

5 - 0 =

Number of Apples

Type of Apple	1	2	3	4	5	6	7	8
Green	🍏	🍏	🍏	🍏	🍏	🍏		
Yellow	🍎	🍎	🍎	🍎	🍎			
Red	🍎	🍎	🍎	🍎	🍎	🍎	🍎	🍎

 Look at the graph.
Write the numbers in the correct boxes.

6

Green apples

Yellow apples

Red apples

GRAPHS

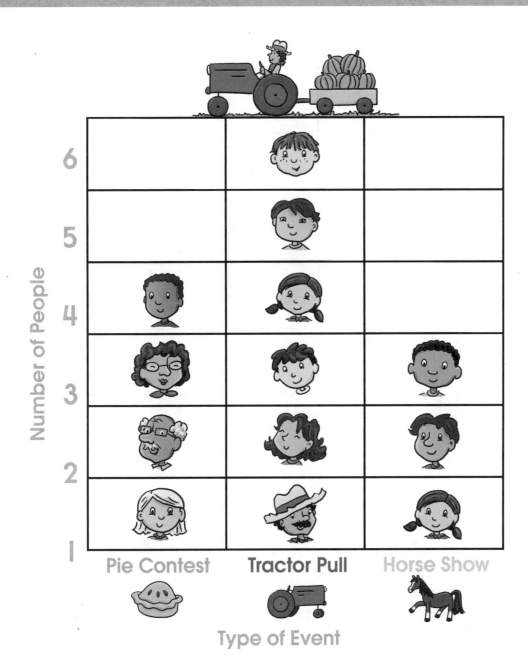

Number of People

6
5
4
3
2
1

Pie Contest   Tractor Pull   Horse Show

Type of Event

Look at the graph.
Write the numbers in the correct boxes.

Pie Contest

Tractor Pull

Horse Show

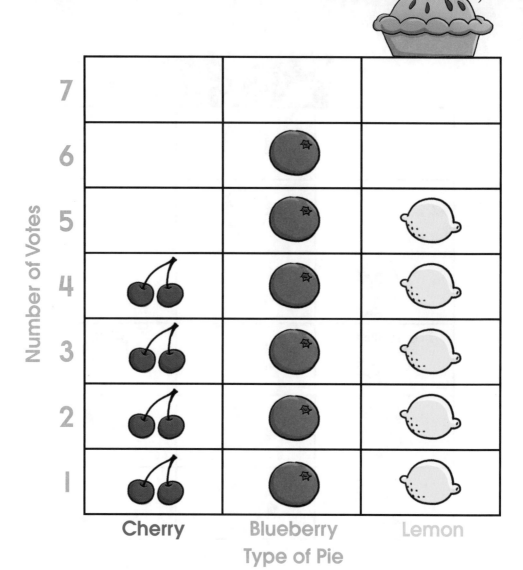

Number of Votes

	7			
6			
5			
4			
3			
2			
1			

Cherry   Blueberry   Lemon

Type of Pie

 Look at the graph.
Write the numbers in the correct boxes.

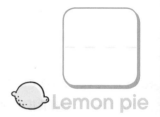

Cherry pie   **Blueberry pie**   Lemon pie

 Circle the favorite pie.

GRAPHS

Count how many are in each group.
Color in the graph.

Number in the Circus	Clowns	Dogs	Pigs	Horses
6				
5				
4	███			
3	███			
2	███			
1	███			

 Clowns   Dogs   Pigs    Horses

Type of Circus Performer

A clock has two hands.
The **short hand** is the **hour** hand.
The **long hand** is the **minute** hand.

3:00

 Read the number the hour hand is pointing to.
Write the time.

_____

_____

_____

_____

TELLING TIME

 Read the number the hour hand is pointing to.
Write the time.

Draw lines to connect the clocks that show the same times.

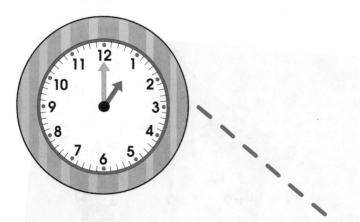

Draw lines to connect the clocks that show the same times.

Look at the time below each clock.
Draw an hour hand on each clock to match.

2:00

5:00

11:00

12:00

How many clocks say **4:00**? _____

How many clocks say **9:00**? _____

The **penny**

front   back

A **penny** is **one cent**.
1 penny = 1¢ = $.01

 How many cents are there?
Write the number.

_____ ¢

_____ ¢

_____ ¢

_____ ¢

 How many cents are there?
Write the number.

_____ ¢

_____ ¢

_____ ¢

_____ ¢

Count the money.
Write the amount.
Circle the number that is **greater**.

_____

_____ ¢

_____

_____ ¢

_____

_____ ¢

_____

_____ ¢

_____

_____ ¢

_____

_____ ¢

SHOPPING

✓ the things you can buy with a penny.

jet
5¢

puppy
4¢

car
1¢

balloon
1¢

doll
1¢

bear
2¢

marbles
1¢

top
6¢

monkey
3¢

ball
4¢

How many toys cost a penny? _____

The **nickel**

front   **back**

A **nickel** is **five cents**.
I nickel = 5¢ = $.05

 =

 Count the money. Don't forget to count by **5**s.
Write the total.

_____

_____ ¢

_____

_____ ¢

_____

_____ ¢

_____

_____ ¢

COUNTING MONEY

 Count the money.
Write the total.

_____ ¢

_____ ¢

_____ ¢

_____ ¢

Count the money.
Write the total.

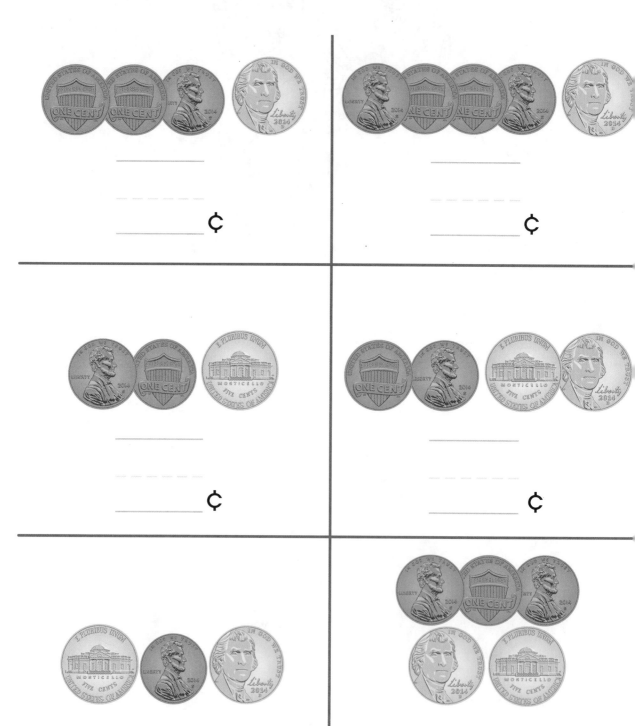

¢

¢

¢

¢

¢

¢

 Count the money.
Write the total.
Circle the number that is **greater**.

_____

_____ ¢

_____

_____ ¢

_____

_____ ¢

_____

_____ ¢

_____

_____ ¢

The **dime**

front   back

A **dime** is **ten cents**.
1 dime = 10¢ = $.10

  =

 =

 =

Count the money. Don't forget to count by **10**s.
Write the total.

_____
_____ ¢

_____
_____ ¢

Count the money.
Write the total.

_____

_____ ¢

_____

_____ ¢

_____

_____ ¢

_____

_____ ¢

_____

_____ ¢

_____

_____ ¢

Equal parts are the same size and shape.
Look at the shapes.
One shape has 2 equal parts.

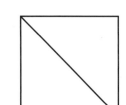 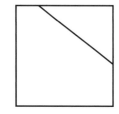

Equal Parts   Unequal Parts

 Circle the shapes that have **equal** parts.

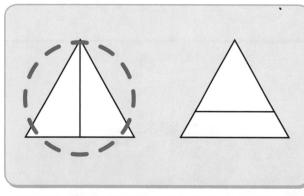 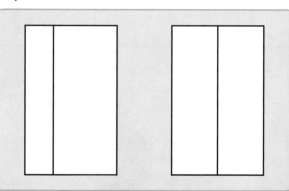

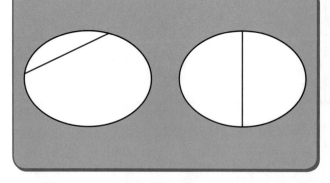 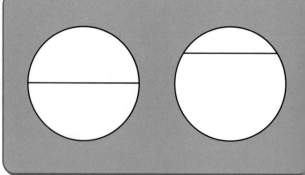

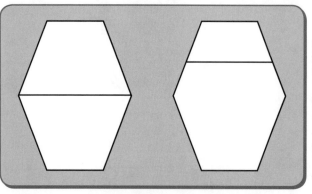 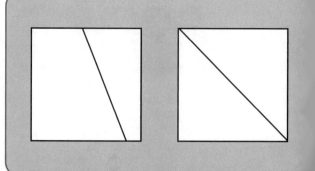

248

Look at the shape. It has 2 equal parts. Each part is **one-half** or $\frac{1}{2}$.

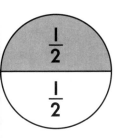

$\frac{1}{2}$ ← parts colored
$\frac{1}{2}$ ← equal parts

$\frac{1}{2}$ is a fraction.

 Write the fraction $\frac{1}{2}$ on each part.

$\frac{1}{2}$

$\frac{1}{2}$

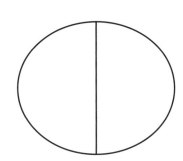

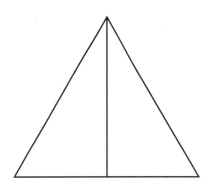

Color $\frac{1}{2}$ of each shape.

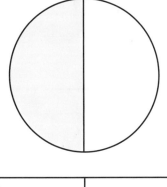

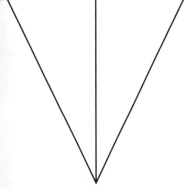

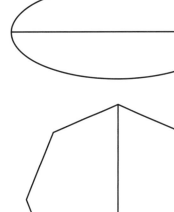

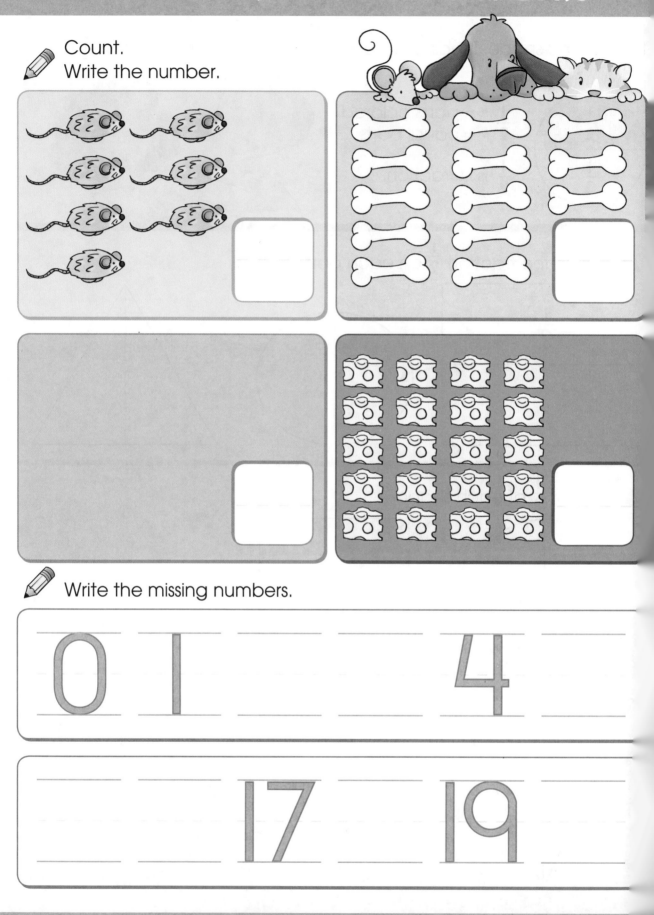

Count.
Write the number.

Write the missing numbers.

0 1 _ _ 4

_ _ 17 _ 19

Write the number that comes **before** these numbers.

```
___ 14 15          ___ 1 2
```

 Write the number that belongs **between** these numbers.

```
9 ___ 11          18 ___ 20
```

 Write the number that comes **after** these numbers.

```
7 8 ___          15 16 ___
```

 Count.
Write the numbers.
Circle the number that is **greater**.

Circle the number that is **greater**.

7   5   16   19   17   15

Circle the number that is **less**.

20   12   17   13   9   0

Color the shape to complete the pattern.

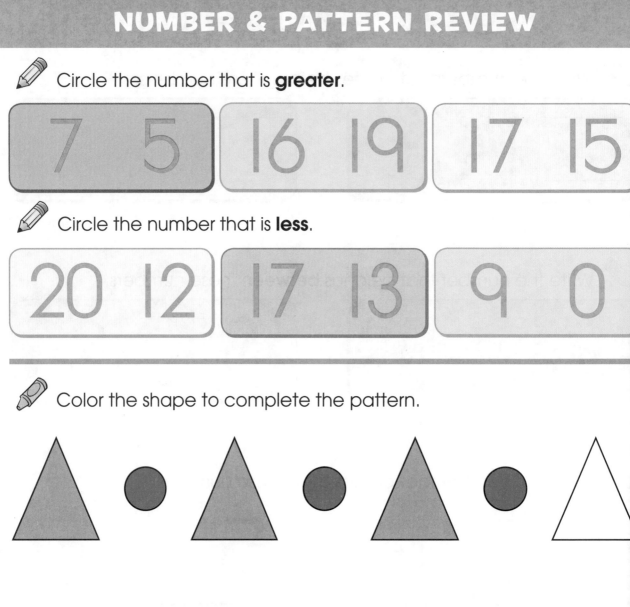

READING READINESS

There is no ability more essential to your child's success in school than reading. Reading, and understanding what is read, is the key to all of the other subjects. This section's activities will build the skills that your child needs to learn to read quickly, easily, and with good comprehension. The activities will help your child practice many important skills, including: observing details, recognizing similarities and differences, matching, comparing and contrasting, classifying, exploring the concept of size, identifying emotions, exploring the senses, understanding weather, identifying opposites, working with positional words, identifying rhyming words, understanding cause and effect relationships, identifying story order, and relating words and sentences to pictures.

These are the **same**.

This is different.

 Circle the picture that is the **same** as the first one.

Circle 2 that are the **same**.

Circle 2 that are the **same**.

LOOK-ALIKE ANIMALS

These are the same.

This is **different**.

 Circle the picture that is **different**.

BUZZING AROUND

 Circle the picture that is **different**.

HOME ON THE RANGE!

 Compare pictures **A** and **B**.
Circle what is different in picture **B**.

Picture **A**

Picture **B**

The girls' mittens are mixed up.
Draw lines to help them find their mittens.

MATCHING

 Draw lines from the clown to the items that he is wearing or holding.

Draw lines to **match** the pairs of socks.

ODD SHOE OUT

 Draw lines between the shoes that **match**.
Circle the shoe that does not have a match.

 Draw a line from each vehicle to the job it does.

ANIMAL HABITATS

Draw a line from each animal to its home.

BASKET OR TOY BOX?

✏️ Draw a line from each picture to where it **belongs**.

Draw a line from each picture to where it **belongs**.

Animals

Plants

SOMETHING DOES NOT BELONG!

 what **does not belong**.

SOMETHING'S NOT QUITE RIGHT!

 what **does not belong**.

✖ what **does not belong** in the tree.

✖ what **does not belong** underwater.

SILLY SWING

 Circle what **does not belong** in the picture.

A SUNNY DAY AT THE BEACH

 Draw faces to show how you would feel. happy sad

 Draw something that makes you .

Draw something that makes you 😟.

Learning about Emotions   272   ©School Zone Publishing Compar

MAKING FACES

 Circle the face you would make.

Draw a line to show which sense each child is using.

The Senses

Smell

Sight

Taste

Hearing

Touch

 Draw lines to match the senses.

Smell   **Sight**   **Taste**   **Hearing**   **Touch**

IT MAKES PERFECT SENSE!

What are some ways people use their senses?

Smell

 Draw something you can smell.

Hearing

Draw something you can hear.

Taste

Draw something you can taste.

Touch

Draw something you can touch.

Sight

Draw something you can see.

WEATHER

snowy   rainy   cloudy   sunny

 Use the calendar to answer the questions.
Circle the correct answer.

What was it like on March 5?	What was it like on March 10?
What was it like on March 21?	What was it like on March 29?

Draw a picture of your favorite kind of weather.

FUN IN ALL KINDS OF WEATHER

 Draw a line to match each type of weather to the correct scene.

The year is made up of four **seasons**.

Spring

Summer

Autumn

Winter

 During which season does each activity happen?
Draw a line to match each activity with the correct **season**.

Spring

Summer

Autumn

Winter

OPPOSITES

 is the **opposite** of closed.

Open

 Draw lines to match the **opposites**.

happy

cold

day

big

small

sad

hot

night

Draw lines to match the **opposites**.

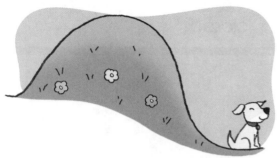

down

off

top

full

empty

up

on

bottom

OPPOSITES

up   **down**

 Draw lines to match the **opposites**.

sad

new

slow

short

old

fast

happy

tall

 Circle the **opposites**.

Where is the bird?

over

under

inside

by

Circle the correct word to finish each sentence.

The is _____ the doghouse.   **over   under   inside   by**

The is _____ the doghouse.   **over   under   inside   by**

The is _____ the doghouse.   **over   under   inside   by**

The is _____ the doghouse.   **over   under   inside   by**

OPPOSITES & POSITIONAL WORDS

high **low** **left** **right**

Color the ⬭ that are **high red**.

Color the ⬭ that are **low blue**.

Color the 🐱 that is going **right orange**.

Color the 🐱 that is going **left black**.

BIGGER SIZE

This 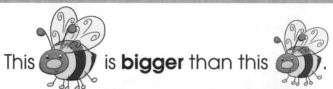 is **bigger** than this.

 Circle the picture that is **bigger** than the first one.

Circle the picture that is **bigger** than the first one.

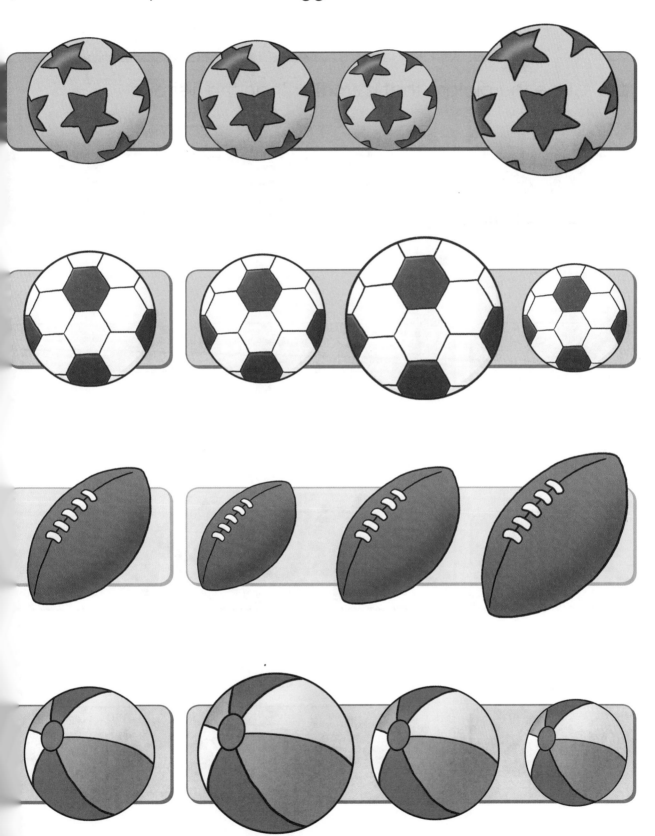

SMALLER SIZE

This  is **smaller** than this.

 Circle the picture that is **smaller** than the first one.

Circle the picture that is **smaller** than the first one.

BIG & SMALL

This is **big**. This is **small**.

Look at the pictures in each row.

 the picture that is the **biggest**.

 the picture that is the **smallest**.

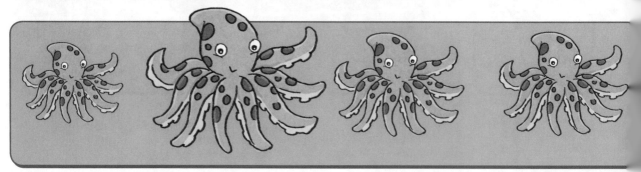

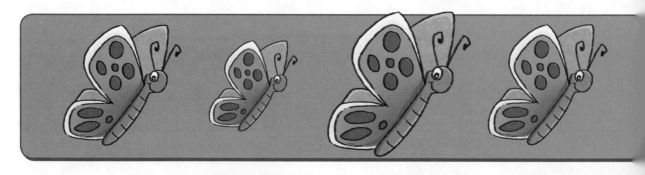

This is **short**. This  is **tall**.

Look at the pictures in each group.

 the picture that is **short**.

 the picture that is **tall**.

ARROWS

left   right   up   down

 Look at each arrow.
Circle the correct word.

(left)
right

up
down

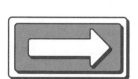

left
right

down
up

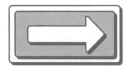

right
left

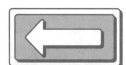

left
right

down
up

up
down

up
down

down
up

right
left

left
right

PREPOSITIONS

inside   outside   on

 Color the animals **inside** the fence **brown**.

 Color the animals **outside** the fence yellow.

 Color the animals **on** the fence orange.

RHYMING WORDS

 rhymes with

Hat   cat.

 Say the name of each picture.
Circle the two that **rhyme** in each group.

mitten

pear

bear

fox   flower

box

bee

tree   lamp

cupcake   nail

whale

RHYMING WORDS

 In each row, circle the pictures that **rhyme**.

cat   hat   fish   bat

apple   house   mouse   ball

coat   crayon   goat   boat

fan   can   pan   pie

RHYMING WORDS

 Circle the word that **rhymes** with the first one.

star

stork

dog

sun

grapes

fork

kite

baby

boat

whale

frog

one

bat

hat

mouse

bee

car

ball

pear

house

Draw a line between the words that **rhyme**.

house

fox

bee

box

mouse

tree

goat

hat

boat

snail

pail

cat

frog

log

Circle the little picture that shows why this happened.

Circle the little picture that shows why this happened.

SEQUENCING

 Write **1** to show what happened **first**.
Write **2** to show what happened **next**.
Write **3** to show what happened **last**.

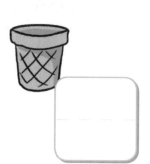

SEQUENCING

 Write **1** to show what happened **first**.

 Write **2** to show what happened **next**.

 Write **3** to show what happened **last**.

SEQUENCING

Write **1** to show what happened **first**.
Write **2** to show what happened **next**.
Write **3** to show what happened **last**.

SEQUENCING

Write **1**, **2**, **3**, and **4** to show each story's order.

Draw lines to match the **action words**.

slide

climb

climb

jump

dig

slide

jump

dig

Draw lines to match the **action words**.

run

hop

swing

fly

hop

run

fly

swing

Underline the sentence that goes with the picture.

I see a ball.

I see a dog.

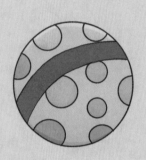

I see a doll.

I see a ball.

I see a boat.

I see a dog.

I see a doll.

I see a boat.

Underline the sentence that goes with the picture.

I see an apple.

I see some toys.

I see a dog.

I see a dog.

I see an apple.

I see some toys.

I see some toys.

I see a boat.

I see an apple.

I see some toys.

I see a dog and an apple.

I see a dog and some toys.

I see some toys and an apple.

I see a dog and an apple.

I see a dog and some toys.

WHAT CAN IT DO?

 Underline the sentence that goes with the picture.

It can run.

It can jump.

It can fly.

It can hop.

It can jump.

It can dig.

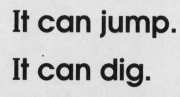

It can hop.

It can fly.

It can swim.

It can hop.

It can fly.

It can dig.

Underline the sentence that goes with the picture.

There is one.

There are two.

It is going up.

It is going down.

It is long.

It is short.

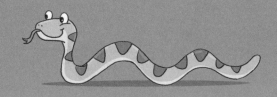

It is going up.

It is going down.

It is big.

It is small.

It is jumping over.

It is jumping under.

Match each sentence to the correct picture.

I am red.

You can ride me.

I am huge.

I come after two.

I am soft.

Underline the sentences that tell what you see in the picture.

There are two horses.

There are four balls.

There is a barn.

There is one goat.

There is a girl.

A **community** is a place where people live and work. Find your way around this community by helping the school bus get to the park.

Town Police Station

Town Bank

Dinah's Diner

Firehouse #1

Grocery Store

+ Hospital +

Emergency

Learning about a Community

Draw a line to match each store with something it sells.

JOIN THE PARADE!

 Draw a line from each child to what he or she is holding.

 Find and circle **6** hidden ladybugs in the picture.

HAVING A PICNIC

 Help plan a healthy picnic lunch.
Draw a food from each food group on the plate.

RECYCLING

Recycling is a way to reuse things and keep our planet clean.
Help clean up after the picnic.
Draw a line from each item to the correct recycling bin.

315 Learning about Recycling

ANSWER KEY

No Answer Key is provided for pages 1–175, 178, 196, 202, and 253–315.

Page 176
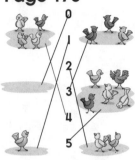

Page 177
3   1
5   0
2   4

Page 179
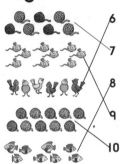

Page 180
5   7
6   9
10   8

Page 181

Page 182
```
0 1 2 3 4 5 6
0 1 2 3 4 5 6
3 4 5 6 7 8 9
4 5 6 7 8 9 10
4 5 6 7 8 9 10
```

Page 183

How many 🐱 are there? ④ 5 6
How many 🐭 are there? ④ 5 6

Page 184
9
8
8
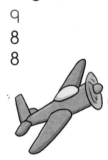

Page 185

5 3
3 2
4 5
10 8

Page 186
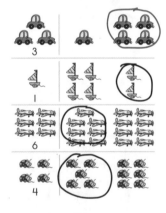
3
1
6
4

Page 187
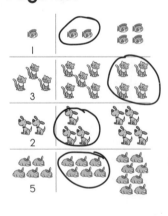
1
3
2
5

Page 188
5
8
7

Page 189
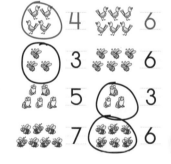
4 6
3 6
5 3
7 6

Page 190
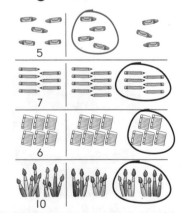
5
7
6
10

Page 191
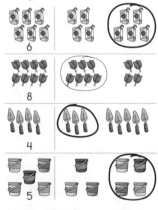
6
8
4
5

Page 192
4
8
10
5

Page 193
2 6
4 8
7 5

Page 194
3 6
5 8
7 9

Page 195
4 8
9 6
10 3

ANSWER KEY

Page 197

12   15
14   13

Page 198

6
4
9

Page 199

Page 200

1
4
6

Page 201

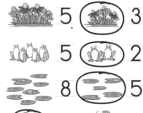

Page 203

17   19
20   18

Page 204

Page 205

12
15
11
17
20

Page 206

16   18
13   9
17   15

Page 207

17   11
19   18
13   16

Page 208

5   20
9   13
2   16

Page 209

5 6 7 8 9 10
7 8 9 10 11 12
3 4 5 6 7 8
13 14 15 16 17 18
15 16 17 18 19 20

Page 210

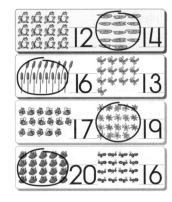

Page 211

13
12
7
10
15
17
9
19

Page 212

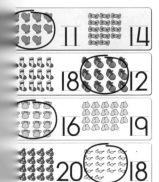

Page 213

9
6
13
15
7
17
19
14

Page 214

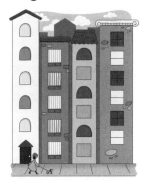

Page 215

ANSWER KEY

Page 216
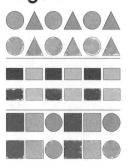

Page 217
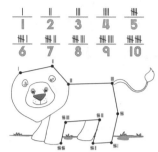

Page 218
I	II	III	IIII	ⵜ
1	2	3	4	5
ⵜI	ⵜII	ⵜIII	ⵜIIII	ⵜⵜ
6	7	8	9	10

Page 219
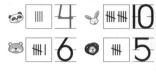

Page 220
2   2
3   3

Page 221
4   4
4   4

Page 222
5   5
5   5

Page 223
6   6
6   6

Page 224
1   1
1   1

Page 225
2   2
2   2

Page 226
3   3
3   3

Page 227
4   4
5   5

Page 228
 Green apples = 6

 Yellow apples = 5

Red apples = 8

Page 229
 Pie Contest = 4

 Tractor Pull = 6

 Horse Show = 3

Page 230
 Cherry pie = 4

 Blueberry pie = 6

 Lemon pie = 5

Page 231
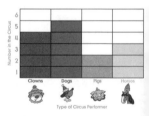

Page 232
7:00   12:00
1:00   10:00

Page 233
9:00   6:00
4:00   11:00

Page 234
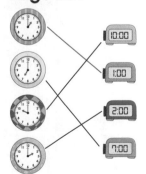

Page 235
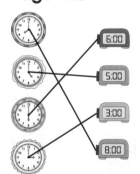

Page 236

2:00   5:00

11:00   12:00

ANSWER KEY

Page 237

How many clocks say 9:00? 8
How many clocks say 4:00? 7

Page 238

5¢
8¢
6¢
7¢

Page 239

7¢
9¢
12¢
14¢

Page 240

3¢ (5¢)
(8¢) 7¢
(12¢) 11¢

Page 241

How many toys cost a penny? 4

Page 242

5¢
10¢
15¢
20¢

Page 243

6¢
11¢
13¢
17¢

Page 244

8¢   9¢
7¢   12¢
11¢   13¢

Page 245

6¢   (7¢)
8¢   (10¢)
(15¢) 12¢

Page 246

10¢
20¢

Page 247

10¢   20¢
11¢   14¢
15¢   12¢

Page 248

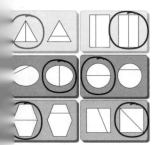

Page 249

Page 250

7   13
0   20

0 1 2 3 4 5
15 16 17 18 19 20

Page 251

13   0
10   19
9   17
13   (15)

Page 252

7 5 16 (19) (17) 15
0 (12) 17 (13) 9 (0)

GREAT JOB!

_____

Name

finished the **Big Kindergarten Workbook**

from

School Zone Publishing Company.